D1248982

# MODELS OF MAN

## Philosophical thoughts on social action

MARTIN HOLLIS

CAMBRIDGE UNIVERSITY PRESS

CAMBRIDGE

LONDON · NEW YORK · MELBOURNE

Published by the Syndics of the Cambridge University Press
The Pitt Building, Trumpington Street, Cambridge CB2 1RP
Bentley House, 200 Euston Road, London NW1 2DB
32 East 57th Street, New York, NY 10022, USA
296 Beaconsfield Parade, Middle Park, Melbourne 3206, Australia

© Cambridge University Press 1977

First published 1977

Phototypeset by Western Printing Services Ltd, Bristol
Printed at the University Press, Cambridge

*Library of Congress Cataloguing in Publication Data*
Hollis, Martin.
Models of man.

Bibliography: p.
Includes index.
1. Man.   2. Social action.   I. Title.
BDH50.H62     128}.3     76–49902
ISBN 0-521-21546-3 hard covers
ISBN 0-521-29181-X paperback

BD
450
.H62

# Contents

LIBRARY
ALMA COLLEGE
ALMA, MICHIGAN

# Preface

The ideal author for this book would be expert in several social sciences before rushing in with reflections. It will become plain that I am far from ideal. Happily I have large debts to acknowledge, especially to Bryan Heading and Quentin Skinner. The former has guided me patiently down sociological paths and the themes of the book have been nurtured in our joint seminar at the University of East Anglia. I am very conscious of owing him more than the text reveals. The latter has been a fount of comment and encouragement and his work on the study of history has been in my mind throughout. My explicit borrowings are only a tithe of what I have gained from him. It is a great pleasure to record my deep gratitude to them both.

My warm thanks are due also to others who have read parts of an earlier version or discussed issues with me, notably to Michael Bloch, Alan Dawe, Gareth Jones, Tony Kenny, Steven Lukes, Nick Nathan, Tim O'Hagan, Alan Ryan and David Wiggins.

I have reused, particularly in chapter 1, some material first published under the title 'My Role and its Duties' in R. S. Peters, ed., *Nature and Conduct* (Royal Institute of Philosophy Lectures, volume 8, 1975), and acknowledge permission to reprint it.

Finally I owe H. A. Simon an apology for stealing the title *Models of Man*, which catches my theme so much better than any I could hit upon. I hope he will accept this piece of poaching as a gesture of admiration for his finely etched monograph.

# 1

## Two models

Recipes for the Good Society used to run, in caricature, something like this –

(1) Take about 2,000 *hom. sap.*, dissect each into essence and accidents and discard the accidents.
(2) Place essences in a large casserole, add socialising syrup and stew until conflict disappears.
(3) Serve with a pinch of salt.

Such recipes have produced many classic dishes in political theory. All take men as they are and laws as they might be (to echo the opening sentence of Rousseau's *Social Contract*) but the exact ingredients vary with the chef. In particular the magic formula for the socialising syrup varies with the analysis of human nature. For instance, if men are essentially greedy egoists in pursuit of riches, fame and honour, then the syrup will be a blend of repression through fear and reward for cooperation. If men are born free, equal and good, they need only to be stewed in Enlightened education amid democratic institutions. If men are by nature the sinful children of God, then a conservative chef will distil his brew from notions like law, authority, tradition, property and patriotism, tinged with distrust of reason. But, whether the cuisine is *cordon bleu*, *rouge* or *sanitaire*, there is always an essence of man and a consequent syrup. The idea that political cookery is wholly an empirical, rule-of-thumb business is a fairly recent one and old-fashioned chefs would certainly retort that Michael Oakeshott, for example, cannot cook. I hope to lend some power to their elbows.

In telling us whom to obey and how to live, political

theories have traditionally tackled three sorts of question. Firstly there are questions of quasi-fact about how men are constituted and how societies function. They ask, for example, how aggressive men are in a state of nature, what needs they must satisfy for self-realisation, what happens when they form groups. I dub these questions of quasi-fact because their use is scientific in intent, while their status remains crucially unclear in upshot. Secondly there are those of normative analysis, which anatomise the concepts of the theory in a way that has implications for social ethics. Examples might be 'What is justice?', 'Are freedom and equality compatible?', 'How does authority differ from power?', 'Does every man have a property in his own person?' Thirdly there are questions of praxis meant to show how theory is to be put into effect. They enquire, for instance, how to educate good citizens, how to distribute welfare benefits, how to create revolutionary consciousness. The three categories of question are not wholly distinct – indeed one aim of an ingenious theory is to interweave them – and they amount together to a way of finding how men interact, how they should interact and how they can come to interact for the best. The point of departure is a model of man and, although some tinkering with the model is allowed by means of fear, incentives, education or kindness, the task is mainly a tailoring job. Society is to be tailored to men as they truly are, with the aid of laws as they might ideally be.

But traditional political theory is dead. Or so we are often told by social scientists, bent on making man a subject for science. The old insistence on an essential human nature gave rise to social theories which were metaphysical and normative. Orthodox modern theories, by contrast, strive to be empirical and ethically neutral. Given the textbook canons of empirical science, models of man become metaphysical posits without utility or justification. Given the stock distinction of fact and value, neither evidence nor theory yields a warranted praxis. The start of wisdom is recognition that there is no essence of man. Human wants and needs are dependent variables, functions of social, psychic or biological forces. The individual is no longer *causa sui* in the explanation of social action. Empiricism has triumphed and traditional assumptions are dead and buried. Or so we are often told.

They are buried perhaps, but certainly not dead. They are buried in the roots of the very theories which purport to reject them and they still act as premises for metaphysical systems with implications for social ethics. There is no dispensing with a model of man. The point is not as contentious as it would have been when logical positivism commanded the stage. Even empiricists are again flirting with notions of essence, metaphysicians have re-emerged as pedlars of paradigms and values prove resistant to Positive surgery. But since textbooks of social science are still confident that we have progressed from religion through philosophy to science, it remains worth saying that older assumptions are not so easily shed. Indeed, they cannot be shed. Every social theory needs a metaphysic, I shall contend, in which a model of man and a method of science complement each other. There is no shirking questions of quasi-fact, of normative analysis and of praxis.

What do I mean by a model of man? I would rather answer indirectly by sketching two rival models which have influenced the study of society since the Enlightenment. One will be fleshed out philosophically in the first part of the book, the other in the second. We shall then ask epistemology to umpire between them. Tactics are best left unrevealed, until we have drawn the models but a word about the relation of sociology and philosophy is called for straight away.

Durkheim remarks at the end of the *Rules* that 'sociology does not need to choose between the great hypotheses which divide metaphysicians'. This strikes me as wholly false, for reasons which will emerge. But it would be equally false to say that philosophy does not need to choose between the great hypotheses which divide sociologists. Both parties have a need to poach and a duty to preach. There is an overlap, too little explored amid the growing division of academic labour but not untrodden. Philosophers and social scientists tramp cheerfully through it whenever they propound theories of human action. So I shall dispense with the usual pieties about the sanctity of each discipline in its own realm. To save needless offence, however, let me add at once that I claim no right to sit

3

in judgement. I am not a social scientist and the line I shall take in philosophy is, at the least, contentious. This book is therefore meant to evoke the philosopher in every sociologist and the sociologist in every philosopher. In echo of Montaigne, 'all I say is by way of discourse and nothing by way of advice. I should not speak so boldly, were it my duty to be believed.'

By way of discourse, then, let us think of a man as a black box, whose inputs and outputs are before us but whose workings are an enigma. We can pose the problem in picture form (see fig. 1). The reader should not try to read too much into the

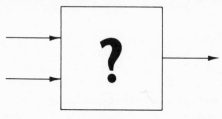

Fig. 1

figure or the two which follow. They are offered solely as *aides-memoire*, perhaps useful if taken lightly but confusing if dwelt upon. None the less let us ask how the box might be filled in. I do not mean how it is to be filled in on some particular occasions of action, since it is a general picture and the inputs are not so much particular stimuli as fundamental processes. The inputs would typically be Nature and Nurture, rather than a door slamming or the arrival of a telegram. Taking the question as a very broad one, we are to fill the box in with a model of men. How many models can be usefully distinguished in this way depends on the purpose of enquiry and the point of view. So, since I propose to pick out just two, I shall impose a simple dichotomy. Social theories will be grouped by whether they treat human nature as *passive* or as *active*. The idea is as old as the problem of free will and loose enough to embrace much of human thought; but it captures a crucial division of opinion in the social sciences and gestures to many concerns of philosophers.[1]

[1] That there are two perspectives on human behaviour in society is a commonplace of sociology, although there are several different accounts of the divergence. The

In pictorial terms, passive conceptions of man give us what I shall call *Plastic Man* (see fig. 2). Plastic Man is a programmed feedback system, whose inputs, outputs and inner workings

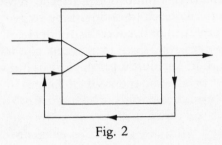

Fig. 2

can be given many interpretations. Active conceptions of man, by contrast, present what I shall call *Autonomous Man* (see fig. 3). Autonomous Man has some species of substantial self within. But what species of precisely what is an open question and nothing should yet be read into the drawing of a little match-stick man inside.

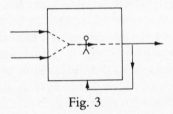

Fig. 3

Even by way of discourse, however, we cannot start with a massive contrast amorphously drawn, and a specific context is needed. Current tensions between passive and active seem to me to stem from the thought of the Enlightenment and I propose to trace the theme from there, before finding examples of them in the social theory of the last few years.

version I shall give reflects the distinction drawn in Alan Dawe's striking article 'The Two Sociologies', *British Journal of Sociology*, 1970, reprinted in *Sociological Perspectives*, Penguin in association with the Open University Press, 1971. Debate between passive and active conceptions is conducted more obliquely in philosophy and many disputes about the explanation of action, the interpretation of experience or the nature of responsibility, for example, bear on it without always being directly addressed to it. But some works which do treat the issue in the spirit defended here are cited in the bibliography.

(Readers who share my distrust of cornflake-packet intellectual history will perhaps grant some excuse for an impressionistic start.) The mark of an Enlightenment thinker is to hold that man is perfectible through science. When this idea is rendered precise, some conflicts in modern attempts at understanding human agency become instructively clear.

Faith in the perfectibility of man can be put, less bombastically and more in keeping with the political theories hailed earlier, as the belief that the laws of human nature can be harnessed to produce a society which satisfies human nature. Breaking the belief down further we find three presumptions, the last of which combines conflicting elements of the others. Firstly, there are held to be, in Hume's phrase, 'constant and universal principles of human nature' (*Enquiries* VIII); secondly, social engineers are deemed to have a power of initiative and innovation, which somehow transcends these constant and universal principles; thirdly, human nature is taken to be fixed enough to have given needs or wants, yet mutable enough for those needs and wants to be satisfiable. These presumptions embody both the models of man, which are our points of departure.

The conflict lies in the interplay between the fixed and mutable elements of human nature. There has to be constancy, partly so that a science of man is possible and partly for the sake of a criterion of progress. If men were wholly unpredictable, they could not be manipulated; if they were wholly pliable, they could be manipulated too easily. It is no part of Enlightenment thinking that freedom and happiness for men could be gained by prefrontal lobotomy. Yet, we may suppose, a cheerful imbecile is conscious of no unsatisfied desires. The objection to utopia through oblivion therefore has to be the loss of human dignity or identity. There have to be needs and wants whose satisfaction is crucial for self-fulfilment. This is a *sine qua non* for an ethic which takes men as they are and for a science which bases the understanding of society on constant and universal principles of human nature. On the other hand progress has to be possible. Since most of our current ills are traced to defects in human nature, there has to be scope for improvement without destroying human identity. Social engineering does not change the universal principles but it alters the initial conditions. Men behave predictably better in an environment better suited to their needs. The social engineer harnesses science and so he has to know what he is doing and have the power to do it. His innovations involve initiative, in an uncompromising sense, as we shall see. There is thus a tension in the basic view of man, who is sometimes puppet and sometimes puppeteer, sometimes passive and sometimes active.

Before we fill out these two models in turn, there is an objection to parry. We began by speaking roundly of an essential nature of man and of separating his essence from his accidents. It will be objected that few theories deal in such essences. Plastic Man, for instance, is surely a creature without an essence, as his name suggests. Indeed Autonomous Man, even if somehow possessed of a self, need not be a scholastic substance. Why confuse the issue in this antiquarian way? In reply, I do not quite mean 'substance' and 'essence' to be taken as part of an ontology of necessary beings and subsistent attributes. But I do mean to stress the presence of some ontology and metaphysics in basic assumptions about human behaviour. Paradoxically, any claim that Plastic Man has no essence will turn out to be an essentialist thesis, in that it asserts *a priori* and on epistemological grounds an informative proposition about the stuff of human behaviour. However, it is too early to deploy the view of scientific knowledge which removes the paradox or makes it more than banal that the man who denies one metaphysic thereby asserts another, and, for the moment, terms like 'essential human nature' are being used somewhat lightly. If the objector will agree that there is some basic distinction between passive and active conceptions of man, I will settle for calling them assumptions.

Now let us attend to Plastic Man. Talk of 'constant and universal principles of human nature' suggests that we are natural creatures in a rational world of cause and effect. This is an Enlightenment theme which has dominated orthodox sociology and it implies that we are objects in nature differing from others only in degree of complexity. 'Man is not fashioned out of a more precious clay; Nature has used only

7

one and the same dough in which she has merely varied the leaven', as La Mettrie put it in *L'Homme Machine*. There is scope for much dispute about how she has done her work, however. Plastic Man has many variants and I impute no simple-mindedness to his proponents. The common factor is more abstract. It is that passive conceptions are naturalistic and deterministic. Neither term is straightforward.

Naturalism is a bland doctrine in its own right, asserting only that whatever is not supernatural belongs to a unitary natural order. Historically, it gets its point in opposition to Cartesian dualism (or, rather, to received interpretations of that doctrine). Descartes, in founding modern philosophy, also founded some of its hardest puzzles. Partly in order to reconcile the duties of a Catholic with the hopes of a scientist, he divided heaven and earth into three substances or orders of being: God, mind and nature. Nature was a realm of matter in motion, governed by iron laws which made the succession of its states utterly necessary and so, he hoped, open to explanation by mathematical methods. Mind was a realm of subjects of consciousness and each self or soul in it had a free will untrammelled by the laws of nature. Borrowing from an older notion of substance, he took each order of being to be a self-contained system whose essential attributes were unique to itself and whose states could all be explained from within. (I ignore the fact that he held all things to be dependent on God, who was thus the only true substance, in order to concentrate on the relation between man and nature.) Natural objects essentially occupied space and therefore mental objects did not; mental objects were essentially conscious and therefore natural objects essentially were not. The plan was to secure nature for science, while saving the divine spark in man. Man was to be, in the words of Sir Thomas Browne, 'that great and true Amphibium whose nature is to live not only like other creatures in divers elements but in divided and distinguish'd worlds'. This great and true Amphibium was caught on a frontier between two essentially different orders of being, one of which included all his physical behaviour and the other all his perceptions, beliefs, intentions and, if you will pardon the anachronism, subjective meanings.

Although empiricism came to replace Cartesian rationalism as the philosophy of nature and although Descartes himself no longer seems a giant in the history of scientific discovery, his role in clearing the road for the natural sciences, while barring it for the social sciences, has been of lasting effect. To put it as mildly as possible the mental workings of a great Amphibium could not be studied by the methods of natural science. Naturalism is, historically, the thesis which, if true, extends nature to include man. Mind and nature form a single system with those features of nature which make it a subject for science. It is thus a negative and bland thesis and does not in itself specify the features. It does not, for instance, commit one to materialism or behaviourism, although these are among the more specific -isms compatible with it. Its sole implication is that there is only one general form of scientific explanation. There is no reason in nature to halt a chain of explanation at any point short of the system as a whole. In particular there is no boundary between inner states and environment or between self and society. The scientist may impose stopping points, because his life is short, his intellect finite, his interests selective or his habitat departmental. But nature is a total system without internal boundaries or *ceteris paribus* clauses. Natural and social sciences attack the same one world with the same one method of validation.

Determinism can be taken as specifying the one form of scientific explanation. It has, in fact, several senses, some of them too broad for this purpose and others too committal. It may save confusion. if we list some of them.

(1) Every event has an explanation.
(2) Every event has an explanation in the same mode.
(3) Every event has a causal explanation.
(4) Every event, together with some other event, is an instance of a natural law.
(5) Every event is the only possible outcome of some other event, being subject to laws which could not possibly be otherwise.

Of these the first expresses only the blankest rationalism (with a small 'r', in that literary sense in which empiricists are rationalists too), and puts no limit on the kinds of explanation there may be. The second puts a limit without saying of what kind. The third looks more tempting but leaves the analysis of 'causation' so open that it is no advance on the second. The fourth is more useful. It picks out the group of analyses which turn on the idea that causal explanation is of the particular by means of the general and it introduces the term 'natural law', which will concern us later. The fifth continues by glossing the notion of a law in terms of a very strong notion of necessity, a distinguished line but no longer a common one and so too specific for our purposes.

Accordingly we shall fare best with the fourth. However, some amendment is called for, partly because we are not concerned here with whether there are random events and elements and partly because there may also be causal explanations for states, conditions, dispositions, processes or objects, depending on the kind of ontology accepted. There is also a case for using a less non-committal phrase than 'natural law' but that had better wait until chapter 3. As amended, then, the sense which asserts just enough is that *every fact which has an explanation is, together with some other fact, an instance of a natural law*. (The 'other fact' will be the *explanans*.) Naturalism and determinism now go agreeably together, combining to assert that there is a unitary law-governed world and that knowledge of it depends on identifying its laws.

The mark of a passive conception, then, is to treat human agency as a natural and determined phenomenon, which does not provide, in Leibniz' phrase, 'a necessary being with which we can stop'. The diagram for Plastic Man simply connects inputs to output by an arrow just like the other arrows, thus emphasising the unity of scientific method and abolishing any ultimate hiatus between the inside and the outside of the box. Apart from any random factors, the creature portrayed behaves predictably in given conditions and can be manipulated by engineering apt conditions. Science is thus ready to guide us to the Good Society, where 'the sun will shine only on free men who own no other light than their reason'.[2] We see

---

[2] These words are taken from Condorcet's *Historical Sketch for the Progress of the Human Mind*, xth stage, where the Enlightenment vision is movingly set down.

the point of Helvetius's remark that 'it matters not whether men are good or bad – law is everything'. 'Ethics,' he adds, 'is the agriculture of the mind.'

But the thought that 'law is everything' contains an ambiguity and hides a problem. It gestures both to the laws of nature as they are and to the laws of government as they might be. The former are constant and universal, the latter are prescribed. Someone must innovate, performing actions not readily explained as instances of a natural law. Certainly most Enlightenment texts allow a free man a power of initiative which comes from the use of reason. Helvetius himself was a thorough determinist but Condorcet, just cited, is more typical in allowing men of reason to transcend the laws of nature. 'Knowledge, power and virtue,' he declares, 'are bound together by an indissoluble chain.' In deference to those who hold that science is ethically neutral, we may ignore the intrusion of virtue but we are bound to wonder how knowledge can give power to Plastic Man. I raise this here not to score an objection, since passive conceptions have several answers which we shall consider later, but to point out how easily Enlightenment thought yields a second and active principle in human nature. Innovation is merely the doing of something for the first time; initiative is a concept with a sharper edge and seems to require a fresh model of man.

By the same token, although Enlightenment theories are discernibly individualistic, Plastic Man is not much of an individual. Within a passive conception each of us is unique only in so far as he is the only instance of the intersection of a complex of laws. If there is also a random element, it is to that extent inexplicable and so, to the Enlightened if not to the Romantic eye, offers no source of individuality. Again I point this out, not to score (especially since recent passive theories are often not individualistic at all) but to introduce the other model. Those who take initiative to be the work of an active individual will now be ready for an active conception of the self.

Plastic Man is a natural creature in a rational world of cause and effect. The antiphonal theme in Enlightenment thought is that we are rational creators in a natural world of

11

cause and effect. With the aid of reason we can master nature, manipulate society, change culture and, indeed, shape our own selves. As a political premise loosely shared by many liberals, socialists, revolutionaries and anarchists, the idea is too familiar to need rehearsal. But the mention of reason indicates a tighter bond than mere enthusiasm for the whole man and one which excludes romantics in the name of science. The key to explaining social behaviour lies in the rational activity of the subject self. The black box is equipped with a rational subject self, which we dub Autonomous Man.

The last sentence puts together three distinct themes, each too perplexing for more than a word of introduction here. There is to be a self, whatever that may turn out to be. The self is a subject, in one or more of the senses which that term can take. It is rationality which marks out man, however rationality is to be construed. We should note at once that the three elements are not always all present, even in active conceptions derived directly from the Enlightenment. Individualism can be disavowed; contrasts between subjects and objects are often declared distracting; rationality is not the only contender. In making Autonomous Man a rational subject self, I am generalising only very broadly and, for the rest, giving warning of the line which I shall endorse myself. Nevertheless the themes harmonise. Whereas Plastic Man, being formed by adaptive response to the interplay of nature and nurture, is only spuriously individual, his rival is to be self-caused. Where Plastic Man is an object in nature, his rival is the 'I' of the I and the Me. Where Plastic Man has his causes, Autonomous Man has his reasons.

The bare idea is that Autonomous Man is the explanation of his own actions. But it derives from more sources than the Enlightenment and can be fleshed out in conflicting ways. The self of popular commonsense and everyday ethics owes something to the theology of the soul and to the metaphysics of substances. At the same time, existentialism has a strong, if more highbrow, attraction and the subject self is often taken to have an existence which precedes its essence, meaning perhaps that it gains its identity from acts of creative self-definition. This strand is prettily caught by Sartre in 'Existentialism and

Humanism' – 'In life a man commits himself, draws his own portrait and there is nothing but that portrait.' Somewhere between substance and pure existent, an individual self takes several forms of active we-know-not-what, for instance in some utility theories of economics, in exchange theory in social anthropology, in phenomenological accounts of schizophrenia. Negatively, these diverse views agree in rejecting the explanation of the inner man in terms of natural laws. Positively, they share only a vague belief in some active principle to be ascribed to each individual. At this stage we can only note the problem – in an active conception of man what is being predicated of what?

To complicate matters further, complaints about the self are not confined to friends of Plastic Man. Among the fashionable theories of 'the construction of reality', there is a distinction between those busy with the social construction of reality and those concerned with the construction of social reality. The latter perhaps have no final quarrel with the old liberal notions of the social contract, whereby it is as if pre-social men with pre-formed needs and desires came together to construct the rules and institutions which define their social world. But the former, with more sense of being truly sociological, include an account of how individual identity is conferred by social interaction. Admittedly critics retort that they cannot have it both ways, since a man whose self is conferred upon him must surely be passive. The objection has force and it must be a moot point whether there is space for a *primum mobile*, whose activity arises neither from some pre-social spark, nor from the imprint of nature nor from the thrust of social factors. But we shall contend later that the truth does indeed lie in this precarious space. So we shall take care not to rule out attempts at a primarily social self in advance.

Autonomy is therefore a hard notion even to introduce, since the theories of the self on offer are diverse and unclear. Accordingly we shall do better to fasten on its claims as a notion of explanation. Philosophers, who are as puzzled as anyone about the self and its identity, are readier to help by analysing the concept of action. A language of action is often distinguished from a language of behaviour. Crudely, agents

13

interpret, reflect, plan, decide, act intentionally, hope, regret and are responsible for their choices; patients are conditioned, programmed and provoked. Less crudely, the contrast of agent and patient can be made out for all areas of life, so that each language has an analogue of everything in the other. There can be active accounts of conformity to norms and passive accounts of ethics. Action is not only cerebral and behaviour is not to be equated with physical response. The difference is not in the scope of the languages but in the claims about reference and explanation. The questions of reference are as old as philosophy. They are, for instance, whether the concepts of both refer and, if so, whether to the same things. Are there intentions and acts of will? Are there drives and instincts? Or are such terms used figuratively? Are the referents of one language primary and those of the other parasitic? Such questions, vague and ill-formed as they are, point to an inevitable demand for an ontology. But I doubt whether ontologies are best tackled directly and I would rather focus on the claims about explanation.

Autonomous Man is to be self-caused and self-explanatory. Naturalism and determinism, as defined earlier, are both to be denied. The language of action must include concepts which give sense to the dotted lines inside the box. Bearing in mind the suggestion that rationality holds the key, we can propose that a man's reasons for acting can explain his actions, without being the cause of them. Suitably worked out, this will imply that not all explanation is in the same mode, namely that of associating cause and effect with the aid of natural laws. We can then make the contrast between the languages one of conflicting modes of explanation. It will still be a further question which mode does in truth explain human interaction but we shall have made the initial problem more tractable by creating a clear duty to supply an alternative to causal explanation. The duty falls most evidently on those who reject all causal explanation of action. But it is no less incumbent on those who compromise with determinism by letting causal conditions and laws explain up to a point. Beyond the point of what is causally necessary but not sufficient, a second mode will be needed for whatever is sufficient.

I may seem to have spoken as if there were some sharp distinction in use between the language of action and the language of behaviour and as if it reflected the distinction of active and passive. That is not what I am after. In practice languages are, of course, used in many ways and embody all sorts of shifting distinctions. Also it would be hotly denied by many that the action language is anti-determinist or anti-naturalist. But I am not trying to describe or analyse our everyday talk nor am I trying to claim that *the* language of action commits anyone to anything. My point is solely that a difference in models of human nature can be instructively expressed by one in the entailments between concepts. The neatest way to assert the existence of Autonomous Man is to claim that human conduct falls under such concepts of *action* as imply that it cannot be wholly explained by causal laws and conditions. Whether what is neat is also fruitful the reader must decide on the evidence of later chapters.

The strength of a passive conception lies in its single mode of explanation and well-worked-out causal models; its apparent weakness in the lack of a self to apply them to. It is tempting to say the reverse of active conceptions. But, in the conspicuous absence of an explanatory account of autonomy, the active self is the merest we-know-not-what. Plastic Man thus starts the contest with so great an advantage that champions of autonomy may be inclined to compromise. I have stated the difference between active and passive as a stark dichotomy, but I have not proved that there can be no continuum and many readers will want a bit of both. Nevertheless I undertake to show that there can be no compromise and to propose a notion of the autonomous self together with its missing mode of explanation. Advocates of co-existence are asked to be patient, along with those who find in passive conceptions a sufficient notion of an innovative self.

We are heirs of the Enlightenment and have inherited both themes. The contrast which I introduced quasi-historically is alive in current attempts at theorising in the social sciences and philosophy. No doubt Enlightenment thought is not the sole source. Some perplexities are older. Some arise from reaction against the Enlightenment. But a historical setting was only used for the sake of clarity and we are now ready to exploit the contrast wherever we find it. To close the chapter I shall offer a few brief examples of the tension between active and passive, which show, I hope, how basic and suggestive is the choice of a model of man.

We might expect that Plastic Man has fared better in generalising subjects interested in typical men, whereas Autonomous Man has flourished in subjects which study particular men without overt reference to general laws. If we looked at it in that way, we would presumably put, say, sociology, biology and economics in the former group and, say, history and psycho-analysis in the latter. But we would then be in a great muddle. There is no distinction between typical and particular men which allows the classification of whole disciplines. Nor can I find merit in a division between arts and sciences or, still more tendentiously, between disciplines which follow the methods of the natural sciences and those which do not. Still less should we accept any presumed division between the routines of matter and the quirks of mind. The central argument occurs within each of the human sciences and it concerns not whether man is a subject for science but what sort of science he requires.

The layman's picture of psychology is of a struggle between stark extremes. On one side are those inclined to treat men as super-rats or super-pigeons, armed with stimulus–response theories and hypothetico-deductive tests for causal regularities. Here is Plastic Man without cavil. On the other are existentialists and phenomenologists, exploring the meaning of the life-world for human actors and loud in rejection of all forms of Positivism. That contrast is strikingly clear, even if there are few pure advocates of either extreme. Elsewhere the conflict shows itself as much within theories as between them. For example Goffman seems to offer his actors a sporting chance of working the system for their own ends by clever choices which exploit the uncertanties of role conflict; yet, in other frames of reference, he views his actors with a thoroughly deterministic eye. Freud started as a neuro-physiologist and his relations of ego, superego and id were in principle mechanical, even if the links were at present unknown. Yet a psycho-therapy, inspired by belief in the power of drives and instincts, offered the patient who understands his repressions a way to take control. Control through self-knowledge seems more than release and adjustment. Throughout the book I have caricatured *homo psychologicus* as a crudely passive fellow, as a notional point where psychology can lock onto sociology. This is a stylistic device and not my ignorant comment on the state of the discipline. Were psychology our topic, an instructive conflict of models of man would leap to the eye.

Economic theories may be roughly sorted into neo-Classical and Classical–Marxian, the difference turning on whether or not supply and demand are analysed in abstraction from social and technological interdependence among the means of production. On the neo-Classical side, our question is raised typically by the lurking presence of a rational individual behind every allocation of resources. On the one hand he is an actor who seeks to maximise his utility by rational choices which bring him nearer to the margin of indifference. His view of his situation is crucial to explaining his behaviour and his actions manifest inner desires and satisfactions. On the other hand there is a marked tendency to a behaviourism, in which revealed preference is sufficient evidence of desire and rationality assumptions are used to eliminate all actual differences between men placed in economically similar settings. Rational economic man is thus lodged in our two frameworks. Similarly, Classical and Marxian theories of political economy hesitate about the identity of their human units. Marx and Engels, for instance, did not say solely that economic forces and relations of production determine the social being of men, which in turn determines their consciousness; nor is 'determination' here a simple or mechanical notion. Dialectical materialism takes as its basic unit a set of agents who, in producing and reproducing their means of life, reproduce themselves. Superstructure is not solely an epiphenomenon. And, if these are complex features of what seems none the less a passive conception, Marxists have always been interested in the causes and cure of alienation. *Prima facie*, at least, alienation is an affliction of the inner man which prevents the victim from

17

being at one with himself, his products, his fellows and his humanity. This reading stands despite the scorn which Marxists usually pour on the mythical individuals invented by Enlightenment liberalism; and there is also a power of initiative attained by the working class or its leaders, when false consciousness is overcome. Notoriously the intellectual tension here has yet to be resolved.

Orthodox sociology has been marked by a long argument between structuralism and actionism, with much manoeuvre on the middle ground. It is easy to take this for a dispute between passive and active. Certainly the bald thesis that social structure determines social action favours the passive side. But it is not often put so baldly as to make men the mere puppets of external structures. Usually the thesis is a limited one, asserting the importance of trends and rates, for example, but allegedly saying nothing about the individual, or else making a restricted claim about what sociology can and cannot tackle and prescribing its proper method of enquiry. Also it is much debated whether or not the crucial structures are normative and those who think they are have commonly kept some place for voluntarism. So there is a tension between active and passive even in the citadels of sociologism, although I shall be arguing that here the passive must prevail. On the other hand it is false that self-styled actionists usually have an active conception. Notions like subjective meaning, symbolic interaction, role-distance or exchange can indeed be used to express a claim about human autonomy and the concept of *Verstehen* can indeed be used in epistemological support. But it is still a novelty and, as we shall see, one which comes to nothing unless *Verstehen* is more than an heuristic device. In orthodox hands these notions have served only to lengthen the causal chain between structure and action, complicating what is still a continuum, because still unified by a single notion of causal explanation. So I shall contend that the long argument, for all its vigour, is deceptive and is not in truth between active and passive. None the less there is a debate between Plastic Man and Autonomous Man, which does disturb sociology at its roots. The line of demarcation falls where 'weak' and 'strong' actionism divide and will give us much exercise later. I

18

shall try to show that the nub is once again the truth about human nature.

There are plenty of other examples but I daresay their purpose would be clear enough already. It matters more to say why a dispute about human nature will turn out to be vital. The reason, as hinted, is that both the identification of a social scientist's data and the proper criteria of scientific explanation hang on it. The cheerful absence of epistemology from the present chapter is therefore no promise of abstention. We shall have to enquire later about causal laws and rational action, about hypotheses and assumptions, about experience and interpretation and about empirical knowledge and metaphysics.

There is a lordly tone to this proposal to survey the social sciences through a philosopher's monocle and I repeat that I am not setting up as any sort of authority. Sociologists, for instance, will no doubt complain of my fondness for role theory to the near exclusion of grander structural approaches and of phenomenology. My defence is not that only role theory matters but that the problems it poses are crucial for the view of explanation taken here. Philosophers may observe that I do not much discuss current thinking in Anglo-Saxon philosophy. But this is not primarily meant to be a didactic book. Its aim is not a comprehensive and fair-minded survey but a way of picking out important philosophical problems in social theory. If it succeeds in that, then perhaps its evident sketchiness may be forgiven and its short way with large and subtle issues taken in the spirit intended.

The book's constructive attempt is to find a metaphysic for the rational social self. The conclusions are strictly to do with making the actions of Autonomous Man a subject for science and are not proposed as a nostrum for all areas. There is still a need for causal laws, even though they do not wholly explain social action; hermeneutics offer much but not all. We shall be working modestly to exploit a gap where partial determinism falls short of complete explanation. So Plastic Man is treated very summarily. Parameters for a passive conception are sketched in chapter 2, which opens with nature *vs.* nurture but concentrates on what they have in common, makes the link between being plastic and being passive and finds a sense in which Plastic Man can be a free agent. Although the strength of the passive case lies in a unitary idea of explanation, there are still problems for the analysis of causation and chapter 3 starts by rejecting Positive accounts. The central puzzle concerns 'natural necessity', which I finally assimilate to conceptual necessity, while holding on to the thought that causal explanation must assign the *explanandum* to its general class.

In chapter 4 social action is set in a context of social positions and roles and a notion of 'normative explanation' is introduced. This is explaining by showing the actor to have done what was required and it is open to a passive conception to adopt it. Yet it suits Autonomous Man too and he starts to appear when we ask how reasons for action relate to motives. Autonomous actors are neither *dramatis personae* nor bundles of traits nor pre-social atoms. In chapter 5, on personal and social identity, they emerge as agents who satisfy strict numerical criteria of identity by rational choice of what *personae* to become. It is an objective matter whether action is rational and one calling for judgement of ends as well as of means. The topic is discussed in chapter 6, which serves as counterpoint to chapter 3. There the notions of purpose, intention and rule offer something but not enough and I conclude that only the actor's good reasons can be deemed to incline without necessitating.

Epistemological debts are paid in chapters 7 and 8 with a defence of rationalism. Language can be understood only if Other Minds are assumed to use it rationally in the main and the assumption has to be justified *a priori*. A moral is drawn for history and the sociology of knowledge. The theme of chapter 8 is that rational action is a skill, whose understanding depends on knowing necessary truths about the rational thing to do. Thus rationalism refers both to the thesis that rationality assumptions are essential to social science and to the distinct thesis that all sciences depend on necessary truths knowable *a priori*. Finally the brief chapter 9 sums up and admits to large, unresolved problems, notably in the idea of context.

A miser, summarising the book by telegram, could do it in

six words. Rational action is its own explanation. But, since some will doubt the meaning or truth of this proposition, while others will quarrel with the sense I shall attach to 'rational', six words seemed too few. So let us press on in earnest by giving the floor to Plastic Man.

# 2

## Nature and nurture

'You can't expect a boy to be vicious till he's been to a good school', remarks one of Saki's characters. As one good school insists, *'Manners Makyth Man'* – not social polish but *mores*, codes, norms, institutions, without which there is no individuality. Yet the same good school has a postern gate which used to be the discreet exit for boys expelled. Carved above it is a tag from Horace, *'Naturam expellas furca, usque recurret'* – you can drive out Nature with a pitchfork but she will be back. The parents may not be amused but the school is relieved of blame. A similar gate and inscription grace the nurture side of the nature *vs.* nurture dispute. It leads into a certain kind of psychology and its use is voluntary and more frequent. Return is allowed, indeed some social psychologists hold season tickets. We might be tempted to suppose the gate also marks the boundary of belief in Plastic Man. I shall start the chapter by arguing that, although the nature *vs.* nurture dispute is genuine, it is not about whether men are plastic.

Nurture is the clearer idea. Durkheim puts this pole starkly enough at the end of the *Rules*, where he writes, 'Individual natures are merely the indeterminate material which the social factor moulds and transforms.' Individual conduct is produced by social facts, external to each individual and constraining him. The constraints are mostly internalised, to be sure, and society could not function, were they not. But internalising is a process of being moulded, not an act of rational assent by the inner man. For any inward state which explains action there is always an external and constraining fact to explain the origin of the inner state.

At the other pole J. S. Mill asserts that 'human beings in

society have no properties but those which are derived from and may be resolved into the laws of the individual man'. (*System of Logic* VI. 7. i.) Social behaviour, norms and institutions derive from the 'thoughts, emotions, volitions and sensations' of individuals. Nurture is the process of placing men so that their characters develop. Development follows 'the laws of the Formation of Character', which are in turn corollaries of the universal laws of human nature grounding all the social sciences.

Neither Durkheim nor Mill holds these rugged views without major qualification; both indeed contradict them in other works. But the slogans are too good to miss. At one pole we have a 'social factor', a systemic whole almost as solid and external to each agent as the world of physical things. At the other we have individuals and, as Mill remarks in another context, although there was never a social contract, it is as if there had been. We start with rival accounts of what there is and also rival theses about the proper form of explanation. Their embattled champions are *homo sociologicus* and *homo psychologicus*, the former seen by the latter as a mere compound, the latter seen by the former as an undifferentiated stuff.

In the same brash way, we can notice much agreement between Durkheim and Mill. Both bid us generalise from experience in order to explain. The first five books of the *System of Logic* apply an empiricism descended from Hume and Hartley to the establishing of truths in science. They bid us start from sensation and advance by inductive generalisation. (I am ignoring the role Mill gives to deduction, as a complication which does not belong here.) Aided by the celebrated Methods of Experimental Enquiry, we are to isolate those constant conjunctions which it is rational to rely on. The tenor is practical, the rubric a sort of Discourse on Method for a world of atomic, contingent phenomena, whose only connection lies in the fact of the patterns they form. When Mill reaches the moral sciences in Book VI, he applies the same rules to the study of man. Lest anyone think men special in nature, he spends a chapter arguing that men are as subject to invariable laws as anything else. His Humean view of Liberty and Necessity is important for what I shall claim to be an irrevocably passive conception and the nub of it is tersely stated –

Correctly conceived, the doctrine called Philosophical Necessity is simply this: that, given the motives which are present to an individual's mind, and given likewise the character and disposition of the individual, the manner in which he will act might be unerringly inferred: that if we knew the person thoroughly and knew all the influences which are acting upon him, we could foretell his conduct with as much certainty as we can predict any physical event (VI. 2. ii).

Yet there are no fatalistic conclusions to be drawn from the social sciences. Correctly conceived, the operations of the will are as genuine as they are predictable. We are free when we will what is in character and 'we are exactly as capable of making our own character, *if we will*, as others are of making it for us'. (VI. 2. iii, his italics.)

Durkheim approaches in the same spirit, although he quarrels with Mill at specific points. Thus he complains that Mill makes the causal bond 'purely chronological', when it should be 'logical', and allows plurality of causes, where there must be uniqueness. Also Durkheim believes that social phenomena have functions as well as effects and that social objects are not reducible to 'other social forces'. But, when it comes to isolating causal laws, he settles happily for Mill's method of concomitant variations, and, like Mill, he is sure that the manner in which a man will act can be unerringly inferred. He too sees no conflict with the idea of free will, correctly conceived, although he is clumsier, seeming to miss the virtues of holding that freedom requires determinism –

Sociology does not need to choose between the great hypotheses which divide metaphysicians. It needs to embrace freewill no more than determinism. All that it asks is that the principle of causality be applied to social phenomena. Again, this principle is enunciated for sociology not as a rational necessity but only as an empirical postulate produced by legitimate induction. Since the law of causality has been verified in the other realms of nature . . . we are justified in claiming that it is equally true of the social world . . . However, the question as to whether the nature of the causal bond excludes all chance is not thereby settled. (*The Rules*, Chapter 5.)

We now have the makings of a standard debate. *Homo sociologicus* and *homo psychologicus* are both plastic creatures, in the sense that their behaviour is the product of antecedent factors which operate in a law-like way. The point of debate is whether the key factors are social or psychological. In either case, there is no threat to freedom but it is for debate whether an assumption of determinism leaves the old teaser open or settles it by reconciliation. Science is agreed to be a search for causal laws but the nature of the causal bond is for debate. I shall take up these points here and in the next chapter. But, since they are familiar fare, I shall stress what I think crucial about them, that they beg the most basic questions of human nature and scientific explanation. Asked to choose between nature and nurture, we are no doubt inclined to have both. But the crucial point is that we are entitled to say, 'Neither'.

To conduct a cosy dispute between nature and nurture, we set out for a compromise by driving the extremes together. How does *homo psychologicus* account for the different forms which an allegedly uniform human nature takes in different places and times? Variety and development surely depend on externals. Natural environment no doubt plays a part – life in a desert full of oil differs from life in a tundra full of bears. But there is surely a social factor too – 'the actual behaviour of individuals towards one another is unintelligible unless one views their behaviour in terms of their status and roles, and the concepts of status and role are devoid of meaning unless one interprets them in terms of the organisation to which the individuals belong'.[1] Unintelligibility aside for the moment, the concepts of status, role and institution are at least very convenient and individuals certainly use them in explaining their own behaviour. Social facts have at least an intermediate claim to be deemed external and constraining.

Yet *homo sociologicus* is under pressure to concede something too. Institutions are not simply given. Why do they stand or change as they do? No doubt external variables like the physical environment and the state of technology take a hand but

[1] As Maurice Mandelbaum roundly puts it in 'Societal Facts', *British Journal of Sociology*, 1955, reprinted in A. Ryan, ed., *The Philosophy of Social Explanation*, Oxford, 1973.

there is also a strong case for 'bringing men back in'.[2] For instance technical innovation in the cotton industry could come about because a high demand for textiles and a low productivity of labour make it seem profitable to invest in labour-saving machinery. This explanation cites the state of technology and presupposes something about entrepreneurial roles and functions. But it works only if there is also a psychological law, that 'men are more likely to perform an activity the more valuable they perceive its reward to be and the more successful they perceive it to be in getting the reward'.[3] Men need social relations but social relations depend on the psychology of men.

A polite compromise is now in the offing. Each party claims the topics for which it has impressive evidence and the remaining ground is for negotiation. In practice, at least, a departmental truce is the commonest outcome. Admittedly it need not come so early or comfortably. The last two paragraphs involved no real concession on either side. Sociology may take a few tricks and psychology still be trumps; or the Oedipus complex may have great power to explain in Vienna and none in the Trobriand Islands. Intermediate variables may be genuine enough and yet no clue to the explanations of the last resort. A compromise may be the commonest outcome but it is not the only one and the evidence is not strong enough to decide the issue.

Nor could it be. Schematically behaviour $B_1$, $B_2$, $B_3$, . . . is to be explained by social factors $S_1$, $S_2$, $S_3$, . . . or by psychological factors $P_1$, $P_2$, $P_3$, . . . (or by a mixture). There might seem to be a conclusive result in some domain if

either $(S_1 \text{ and } P_1) \rightarrow B_1$ or $(S_1 \text{ and } P_1) \rightarrow B_1$

$(S_1 \text{ and } P_2) \rightarrow B_1$ $(S_1 \text{ and } P_2) \rightarrow B_2$

$(S_2 \text{ and } P_1) \rightarrow B_2$ $(S_2 \text{ and } P_1) \rightarrow B_1$

But there would be no duty to admit defeat. A lurking $P_3$

---

[2] I borrow the line of thought in this paragraph from G. E. Homans' classical article 'Bringing Men Back In', *American Sociological Review*, 1964, reprinted in A. Ryan, *op. cit.*, and the cotton example with it. D. Wrong, 'The Oversocialised Conception of Man in Modern Sociology', in L. Coser and B. Rosenberg, eds., *Sociological Theory*, London, Macmillan, 1964, is a similarly instructive plea for a whiff of *homo psychologicus*.

[3] The phrasing gives the 'law' a hollow sound but it is Homans' own.

remains possible in the first case, a lurking $S_3$ in the second, to explain the *explanans*. Perhaps the Oedipus complex does not grip the Trobriand Islands, where mothers and maternal uncles take much of the fathers' role, but the Freudian has several cards to play. He can dispute the evidence, find the complex in some translated form or give a psychological explanation of its failure to emerge. When the stern voice of Popper asks, 'Under what conditions would you give up your hypothesis?' both sides can answer without fear of being caught out in practice.

My point is not that the issue is spurious or unimportant. Homans calls it the most general intellectual issue in sociology[4] and any actual distribution of duties between psychology and sociology will affect all actual explanations offered. My point is that it is not the sort of issue which testing can settle. Let us pause on B. F. Skinner's theory of operant conditioning (or something like it), which accounts for behaviour in terms of a history of reinforcement. Thus very young creatures emit behaviour at random, some of which the environment rewards. (The mewling infant's 'ma' is met with an admiring hug.) Reward reinforces response when the stimulus is repeated. The infant learns to select out the exact stimulus and the exact reponse. The reward can be transferred – from a hug to a hug and a word of praise and then to a word of praise alone – and become internalised. In humans the process produces self-monitoring adults, able to function in a complex, often abstract, environment and to train a new generation. In principle all human practices, and so all institutions, can be claimed explicable in this way. *Homo psychologicus* is fast made ontologically simple, epistemologically tidy and methodologically pure.

At first blush we have a theory here which allows empirical predictions of output on the basis of input alone. We can train pigeons to peck levers and children to stack bricks. We can in principle state the conditions needed for a community to function as in *Walden Two*. Whether a Skinnerian theory does at least as well as, say, a Freudian one seems to be a matter of whether operant conditioning does in fact have the results

[4] *loc. cit.*, the opening paragraph.

predicted. On reflection, however, experience is bound to be ambiguous, as soon as the meaning of stimulus and response for the subject makes a difference. With meaning and response classified by what the subject takes them to be, there is always another hypothesis also at stake, to the effect that the test is decisive. We have (a) the general hypothesis that a reinforced response is likely to be repeated for the same stimulus and conditions, (b) a particular hypothesis that $S_1$, reinforced, produces $R_1$, (c) a hypothesis that the stimulus on the occasion of testing is indeed $S_1$, and that the response is (or is not) $R_1$. Having decided the truth of (c), we could no doubt confirm or disconfirm (b). But knowing the truth of (c) depends on having already established some hypothesis like (b); and the failure of (b) is no threat to (a). To take an example (one too cursory to bear weight and meant only as a pointer), the particular hypothesis might be that racial contact reduces racial tension. There would be an apparent counter-instance, if a black ghetto community were dispersed through a white housing estate and frequent violence between blacks and whites resulted. But it would have to be true that the violence occurred *because* the blacks were black and the whites were white. It would also have to be true that the violence increased rather than reduced racial tension. Criteria would be needed for identifying racial tension, its increase and decrease. These criteria would depend on identifying previous cases and each case depends on the criteria which they jointly establish. In the subtle web of alternative interpretations the usefulness of the concept of reinforcement is not at issue. Empirical predictions thus take an importantly restricted form. Assuming that (a) is true, we can set out to correlate $S_1, \ldots, S_n$, with $R_1, \ldots, R_n$ and can apply some criterion of overall economy to decide when to reject a hypothesis that $S_1$ is correlated with $R_1$ and when to reject the test conditions. But (a) is never at stake. To cut a long tale short, it belongs where Evans-Pritchard puts the Zande king's oracle –

Witchcraft, oracles and magic form an intellectually coherent system. Each explains and proves the others. Death is a proof of witchcraft. It is avenged by magic. The achievement of vengeance-magic is proved by the poison oracle. The accuracy of the poison-oracle is determined by the king's oracle, which is above suspicion.[5]

The missing parts of the tale will be found in the next chapter, where grand theory will be further compared with the king's oracle and middle-range theory with the poison oracle. Skinner is not being singled out, when I assert that his central hypothesis is not testable. Talk of paradigms is in fashion and, if there is anything in it, we should not be surprised to find all tests being predicated on the truth of general presuppositions, unassailable within the paradigm. None the less kings' oracles can come under other sorts of suspicion and I pick Skinner for a second reason. He seems to contradict the idea that every social theorist needs a model of man. Thanks to his behaviourism, his men are so plastic that they seem not to be there at all. I shall use this (mistaken) thought to bring out what I mean by Plastic Man.

We have spoken as if 'nature vs. nurture' were a catchy title for a discussion of psychologism and sociologism. But Skinner represents a psychological case for nurture against nature and we must be less naive. It is one question whether human behaviour is to be traced to something innate in men, as individuals or as a species, and another whether the predicates of the last resort are psychological or sociological. I am not trying to settle the latter question and what I say about it is purely for the sake of the former. Accordingly it will appear as if a claim that men are plastic involves a denial that there is anything innate in them; and hence as if *homo sociologicus* were plastic, whereas *homo psychologicus* were not. This would be unfortunate, especially since Skinner is not the only psychologist who rejects an apparatus of instincts, drives and subconscious givens. Nor am I trying to contrast plastic men with men driven by instincts and drives. For my purposes, a claim that men are plastic is a claim that all determinants of conduct are external to the agent-*an-sich*. The last two words must remain obscure for the moment but the idea is an old one. It is that, like genes, innate psychic factors are antecedent

[5] E. Evans-Pritchard, *Witchcraft, Oracles and Magic among the Azande*, Oxford, 1937, p. 476.

programming devices and therefore that the agent, whose conduct is to be explained, is the creature of a programme he did not write. (In some ways 'Causally Determined Man' or 'Passive Man' would catch the idea better but both would beg questions which I prefer to leave open for the time being.)

Whether there is something innate in men is also an ambiguous question. On one reading it has to do with whether there are instincts and drives. But I mean it in a different sense, which brings out a latent essentialism even in purportedly empirical theories of conduct. Thus Skinner's black boxes are far from empty or as if empty. There are appetitive creatures inside, whose perceptions of environment, stimulus, response, consequences and reward are crucial. Or so it has been persuasively argued by critics.[6] If the comment is fair, there is a richer model of man at work than the claims for a complete technology of behaviour allow. But, even if it is unfair, behaviourism is itself still an essentialist thesis about human nature. For, given that it is untestable and makes a difference to the particular hypotheses offered and accepted, it states *a priori* what categories should be applied in the final explanation of human action. That action does fall under these categories is thus a fact of experience which experience is bound to confirm.

Although Skinner makes men plastic, it is not because he is a behaviourist. Instinctual theories also place the determinants of action outside the control of the agent. So do theories which endorse Durkheim's belief in external and constraining social facts. When we ask exactly what these disparate approaches share, we may be tempted to point to their lack of interest in 'subjective meanings', the rich currency of inner consciousness crucial to all forms of actionism. Accordingly we may be tempted to oppose Weberian notions of meaning and action to all variants of Plastic Man so far mentioned. And indeed Weber's ideas are at odds with the others and are justly included in the Old Testament of Autonomous Man. But 'subjective meanings' are not automatically the currency of a rival model of man. Weber himself seems to have seen them as an explanatory stock, imposed and ordered by some kind of

---

[6] For instance Charles Taylor puts the point with great force throughout *The Explanation of Behaviour*.

31

central value system which is also the ground of Durkheimian social facts. For each actor they are external and constraining, or, if they are not, then they are the effect of something which is. Such an account differs importantly from Durkheim, Mill, Freud and Skinner but not by denying that men are plastic. Weberian meanings, like Freudian interpretations, seem in the end to be treated as ways of filling in causal connections. There is a many-handed dispute about where explanation rests but not about the kind of connections involved.

Any theory makes men plastic, to my mind, if it regards action as the effect of causal antecedents, working in a too law-like manner. This claim will be defended in the next chapter but I assert it here to explain why I have tried to bypass the large disputes between the nature and nurture, between psychologism and sociologism, between behaviour and meaning, between action and structure, between individualism and holism. Some of these disputes will reappear, when we turn to action in earnest. But our present business is with passive conceptions of man. There are two claims. One is that causally determined men are plastic men and we shall try to make it good when we have tackled causal explanation. The other and more contentious is that causally determined men are passive. Durkheim is right to call the issue one of 'the great hypotheses which divide metaphysicians' but, I shall submit, wrong to think that the social sciences can shirk it.

In the passage from the *Rules* just cited Durkheim offers metaphysicians a choice between free will and determinism; whereas sociology need only accept the principle of causality as an empirical postulate, leaving open the question as to whether the nature of the causal bond excludes all chance. If he means that, where the causal bond holds, there is no free will, then he has indeed made his choice. Once free action has been equated with chance action, there is little left to say. Some romantics have been content, in the belief that free action is spontaneous and so unpredictable and so in the realm of chance. But the price is to make free action inexplicable and, conversely, to make explicable action unfree. By this account every advance in social science further destroys our illusions of freedom and so further confirms an atavistic distrust of the scientific enterprise. Durkheim's own words suggest that he does think freedom an illusion or, at best, a residual mystery of no interest. But it is a high price to pay for the hope of progress.

Unromantics will therefore prefer Mill's line, which has chance exclude freedom and puts free action in the realm of causality.[7] Within the class of caused actions, we are to distinguish between the compelled and the free. The line catches our habits of thought well enough, as we divide shoplifters from kleptomaniacs, pianists from pianola players, sane men from psychotics. We act freely, says Mill, when we act predictably in character, having formed our own character as we would ideally wish it to be. 'And hence it is said with truth that none but a person of confirmed virtue is free.' (*System of Logic*, VI. 2. iii.) Hence also, progress in science extends our freedom by teaching us how to form our own characters and to translate desire into action.

But a puzzle remains. Action, as conceived by Mill, results from motive, from character and disposition and from influences, which include the occasion and any standing conditions. Thus a man might commit suicide from a motive to escape dishonour, a characteristic adherence to the Bushido code and the circumstances which thrust the choice upon him. All the elements in the explanation are antecedents which work in a law-like way. The agent does seem to be conceived as wholly passive and the problem is still why his suicide should be deemed a free action. Mill tries three answers. One, quoted earlier, lies in his assertion that 'we are exactly as capable of making our own character, *if we will*, as others are of making it for us' (VI. 2. iii, his italics). Suicide was freely chosen not so much at the moment of action as at the earlier decision to be a man who would respond to such circumstances by suicide. But the puzzle stands, since the earlier decision was presumably itself predictable and Mill gives no clue to the special act referred to in the phrase '*if we will*'. Hence willing

---

[7] Other distinguished proponents have been Hobbes, in *Leviathan* (see also his letter to the Marquis of Newcastle in volume IV of the Molesworth edition pp. 272–8), Spinoza in the *Ethics*, Hume in 'Of Liberty and Necessity' in the *Enquiries* and more recently the Logical Positivists with A. J. Ayer as a famous spokesman in 'Freedom and Necessity' in his *Philosophical Essays*, Macmillan, 1954.

one's own character is either a sort of mental tossing of a coin or a regular process as traceable to its antecedents as any other. While it sounds neat to map free *vs.* compelled onto willed *vs.* unwilled, nothing is achieved, when all have equally law-like determinants.

Nor is anything achieved if willed actions are made exempt from causality. That has already been asserted. Nevertheless Mill relapses later in chapter 11 of Book VI, when he comes to Great Men. The process of history is broadly determined by 'general causes' but men act, he has said earlier, from 'partial causes' also, and prediction of human affairs can only be statistical. 'Great men and great actions are seldom wasted: they send forth a thousand unseen influences more effective than those which are seen.' (VI. 11. iv.) Indeed, 'if there had been no Themistocles, there would have been no victory of Salamis' *(ibid.)*. Whether or not a belief in Great Men can finally be squared with determinism, Mill is here giving them a power of initiative which chimes with what he says of Socrates in *Utilitarianism*. Unlike 'general causes', 'partial causes' seem peculiar to certain individuals, those who would rather be men dissatisfied than pigs satisfied and are rational and strong willed enough to influence history for the better. The *Essay on Liberty* contains a fuller portrait, together with a view of freedom which will turn out to make the free man autonomous. But none of this belongs in the present chapter. From the standpoint of determinism, 'partial causes' are causes and it can only be an aberration to exempt free action from causal explanation.

Thirdly Mill stresses that, correctly conceived, the doctrine called Philosophical Necessity involves no necessity. The laws of psychology, like all other laws, hold universally but not necessarily. Hence, in finding an action a cause, we learn why it was done but we do not show that it had to be done. So there is no conflict between free choice and causal explanation. Necessity would indeed exclude choice but choice presupposes causality. Like many other empiricists before and since, Mill puts his trust in a Humean analysis of cause. If he is right, it is good news for Positive social science, since it blesses the usual pious union between freedom and progress. The more

34

causal laws we find, the better we understand how to get what we want. But I doubt whether he is right. Two striking features of a Humean account of causal explanation are that the explanation of the particular event lies in the general causal law and that the effect of a cause is also the effect of the cause of the cause. These features have nothing to do with whether causal laws hold necessarily or contingently, certainly or stochastically.[8] If there is a query in the first place about how suicide, viewed as the law-governed product of its antecedents, can be a free act, then it arises because the decision is no less the result of its antecedents than the act is of the decision. However strong or weak the kind of necessity involved in the laws and links, it is still true that the decision could have been different, had the conditions been otherwise, and false that it could have been explicably different, while they were the same. Sociologists take pleasure in explaining suicide, because it seems so peculiarly a private and individual choice; but their pleasure is in finding a social law, where others had supposed the law to be of another sort. By the same token, the stock distinction between free and compelled – between, for instance, shoplifters and kleptomaniacs – is only one of common speech. Both categories are equally law-governed and, if there is a puzzle, it springs from that fact alone, regardless of the species of necessity in laws.

The wise determinist, in my view, therefore denies that there is a problem. It is not the will which is free but the man. The man does not so much choose freely, as act freely. For choice is the emergence of effective preference out of a conflict of preferences and effective preference is action. So a man acts freely when he gets what he wants because he wanted it; and freedom is the power to satisfy emerging desires. A man acts under compulsion when he does what he does not want to do, either because there are constraints external to him or because his desires conflict. But compulsion is simply a name for a lack of power, a sign that the agent has no effective desire or none whose exercise has his own approval.

---

[8] It is noteworthy that Hobbes and Spinoza, who use the very same arguments to show that freedom presupposes determinism, maintain that there is a very strong necessity to causal laws.

Such a line has many implications. It takes us into the philosophy of mind, to analyse the difficult notion of desire. It leads on to a political theory of freedom, with a free society as one which minimises the gap between wanting and getting. Were we trying a full-length study of Plastic Man, there would be a huge task ahead. But the modest aim of this chapter is to point up the distinguishing marks of a passive conception and we have yet to discuss in what sense Plastic Man is an individual. The moral so far, then, is that Plastic Man does tangle with metaphysics, in particular the metaphysical question of free will; that the line offering most is the one which has freedom presuppose determinism; and that the price of it is to interpret choice as the translation of desire into action and freedom as the expression of ordered effective preferences.

To broach the question about the agent as an individual, let us recall neo-Classical micro-economics. Here we are offered a sovereign consumer, a rational economic man, portrayed as a translator of preference into action. His tastes are given, or at least determined externally to the model, and he enacts some or all of them according to their opportunity costs at current prices. Diagrammatically he is a set of marginal comparisons between pairs of items, each comparison being expressed in indifference curves –

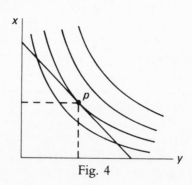

Fig. 4

For a given price (the diagonal line), he maximises his satisfaction at the point tangential to the price line, a point lying on the furthest curve from the origin which the line cuts. The combination of $x$ and $y$ he opts for is thus predictable, given his tastes, the market conditions and the assumption that he is rational. An indifference map portrays a rational fellow with transitively-ordered, irreflexive preferences, subject to a law of diminishing marginal utility.

What is the force of making him rational? The assumption has to do partly with prediction and partly with the notion of agency. Its relation to prediction is a matter of dispute, depending on whether it is taken as asserting that men are rational (either an empirical hypothesis or an *a priori* guarantee) or as specifying how to act rationally (and so making the model prescriptive). I mention this only to put it aside for later. Rationality assumptions also serve as a gloss on the notion of action, however, and the gloss is ambiguous. On the one hand they can be used to eliminate the agent altogether, by guaranteeing a smooth fit between changes in price and effective preferences at the margin. This is the, so to speak, plastic interpretation, making the agent the creature of market conditions. On the other hand they can be used to stress the need for an agent whose map it is. This ambiguity will allow us to argue that Plastic Man is passive, where his rival is active.

Were the map drawn by taking $x$ and $y$ as goods (or, rather, services of goods) given in advance and the curves as the relation between them for any rational man with suitable tastes, it would be a 'passive' map. (I do not mean static, as against dynamic; it can be treated dynamically by including it in a time-series.) We could then contrast it with a map where $x$ and $y$ were the goods they are in virtue of what they meant to the agent, as if this turned the map into an 'active' one. But, as we have seen already, an appeal to the agent's perceptions and reckonings is not enough to distinguish passive from active. There can still be a thoroughly determinist account of the inner man. The contrasting conception must also explain the agent's choice in a different way. To dub him a rational agent is to assert not that he exemplifies the causal laws of economics but that he acts from good reasons. Being at '$p$' is his solution to a maximising problem, rather than the effect of a market change on a creature with his tastes.

Later in the book we shall fill the huge gap produced by

claiming that, when rational action is conceived in an active mode, reasons are not causes. Our present task is solely to set a limit to the scope of passive conceptions, a limit which makes it proper to call them passive. One way to read an indifference map is as a causal explanation of the effects of a price change on a rational agent. The explanation consists in finding a general law to which all rational agents do in fact or, in some nomological sense, must conform. 'Rational' is a predicate picking out a relevant class, rather as the behaviour of a washing powder depends on whether the agents in it are organic or inorganic. The upshot is to put economic behaviour within the scope of a search for causal laws by explaining differences between agents by differences in their properties. Whether or not the agent's world is viewed from within, the explanation of his marginal adjustments lies in the external situation acting through general laws. It seems to me fair to call this a passive conception of rational economic man.

Plastic Man, then, is causally determined within a limit set only by any random element. His actions are to be explained as instances of intersecting laws. What cannot be explained in this way cannot be explained in any other. So there is no room for a compromise between science and the individual which confines science to probabilistic laws and allows individual freedom the balance. Nor is there a compromise whereby science deals in rates, like the suicide rate, and the individual is left to find his own reasons for committing suicide. Only two lines are open. One is to deny Plastic Man all freedom of action, declaring him passive without further ado. The other is to interpret the notion of free action so as to show it explicable by causal laws, with the attraction that freedom will turn out to presuppose determinism. I have not tried to examine the latter line in any depth and some options I have left open may very well be closed on further reflection. Nor have I considered the case for holding that action conceived passively is not truly *action*. For, whatever might be urged against behaviourism, there are subtler ways of applying a framework of causal laws. But the case will be reopened later. So far, I presume that analogues of notions like choice are available but that they are indeed analogues, equating, for instance, choosing with want-

38

ing, being free with being able, 'could have done otherwise' with 'would have done otherwise, if . . .'.

Peter Berger ends his beguiling *Invitation to Sociology* with the image of the puppet theatre –

We see the puppets dancing on their miniature stage, moving up and down as the strings pull them around, following the prescribed course of their various little parts. We learn to understand the logic of this theatre and we find ourselves in its motions. We locate ourselves in society and thus recognise our own position as we hang from its subtle strings. For a moment we see ourselves as puppets indeed. But then we grasp a decisive difference between the puppet theatre and our own drama. Unlike the puppets, we have the possibility of stopping in our movements, looking up and perceiving the machinery by which we have been moved. In this act lies the first step towards freedom. And in this act we find the conclusive justification of sociology as a humanistic discipline.[9]

It would be comforting to sound the same note, before turning to the logic of this theatre in chapter 4. For we have indeed found a difference between the puppets and ourselves. But it is not a decisive difference. In crucial ways we are too like puppets to justify sociology as a humanistic discipline. Conceived as plastic creatures, men are individuals only in so far as they instance different sets of laws. There is, as yet, no general argument about the logic of the theatre but only about the kind of laws which provide the explanations of the last resort. The puppets who perceive the machinery are still puppets and no sense attaches to the idea that the social sciences might cut all their strings. If it is Autonomous Man we want, we shall find him not by deciding between *homo sociologicus* and *homo psychologicus* but by construing the logic of the theatre in a fresh way altogether. That is no doubt why B. F. Skinner thinks that, 'Autonomous Man serves to explain only the things we are not yet able to explain in other ways.'[10] We shall accept his challenge. But first we owe Plastic Man a suitable method of explanation.

[9] Penguin, 1966, concluding paragraph.
[10] *Beyond Freedom and Dignity*, Penguin, 1973, Chapter 1, p. 20.

# 3

# The regularity of the
# moral world

Condorcet wrote in 1794, 'The sole foundation for belief in
the natural sciences is this idea, that the general laws dictating
the phenomena of the universe are necessary and constant.
Why should this principle be any less true for the development
of the intellectual and moral faculties of man than for the other
operations of nature?'[1] In similar vein, Buckle speaks of the
'undeviating regularity of the moral world', which is part of
'one vast scheme of universal order'.[2] These sentiments catch
what I take to be central to passive conceptions, the idea that
human action is a natural and determined phenomenon. Our
next task is to find the best account we can of causal explanation. Naturalism is the thesis that there is only one mode of
explanation, and determinism the thesis that any fact which
has an explanation is, together with some other fact, an
instance of a natural law. It is therefore vital to understand the
notion of a law. I shall present the task as one in epistemology.
What is a natural law and how do we know when we have
found one?

I grasp these nettles in hope, since I do not at all deny that the
moral world has its regularities. Action has antecedents which
sometimes wholly and always partly determine it in accordance with natural laws. My doubts about the orthodox rubric
for social science will not be followed by a rampage in hermeneutics. None the less I accept neither naturalism nor determinism. To explain $x$ is to find a $y$ such that $x$ *because* $y$.
Sometimes '$x$ because $y$' is equivalent to '$x$ is caused by $y$', but,
I shall argue, not always. The equivalence holds for Plastic

[1] *Sketch for an Historical Picture of the Human Mind*, xth stage, 1st paragraph.
[2] *History of Civilization in England*, 1857.

Man but not for Autonomous Man, whose actions will be presented later as wholly explicable but only partly determined. A lesser aim of the chapter is to destroy any presumption that 'because' is always causal.

The job of epistemology, in Kantian terms, is to show how scientific knowledge is possible. On the one hand we have beliefs about the world's furniture and how it works, on the other we have criteria which beliefs must meet to be justified. It is all too easy to assert in ontology what, as epistemologists, we could not possibly know to be true. Thus it is easy to think of causes making effects happen, pushing them into existence or producing them or of natural laws as operating with a real necessity; and to hold at the same time that the limits of possible observation are the limits of science. If we do, then something must give and I shall start by trying to settle the balance in favour of observation. To be precise, I shall begin with a Positivist theory of knowledge and ask what account of causes and natural laws it yields. Readers, warned by the Kantian note just struck, may fear that I am about to put up an Aunt Sally. It is hard not to, seeing that nowadays the verb 'to be a Positivist' appears to lack a first person singular for its present tense; but I intend no mischief. If positivists are goats, it does not follow that Kantians are sheep and I mean only to identify some pressure points for the sake of the soul-searching which is everyone's concern at present.

'Positivism' is often used by philosophers to refer to Logical Positivism, the hard-headed empiricism of the Vienna Circle. For sociologists it conjures up a looser band of heroes as diverse as Comte, Durkheim, Weber and sometimes even Marx. Is there really a single -ism, which makes bedfellows of Carnap and Comte? The *International Encyclopedia of the Social Sciences* thinks not, distinguishing flatly between a nineteenth- and a twentieth-century version and so, admittedly, stopping a riot of confusions.[3] But there is also, I submit, an enduring core to the history of the social sciences. It has to do with the attempt to divide traditional from modern thought by asserting that the limits of empirical science are the limits of possible

---

[3] Arthur Kaplan's article on 'Positivism'.

knowledge of the world. The rest is a matter of how tightly empirical science is defined. In the flush of the Enlightenment it included whatever was the subject of rational belief, of probable judgement and so of progress. Science was the newer name of Reason, a realm which belonged to all rationalists, in the slightly literary sense embracing empiricists too. Mathematics and ethics were still proper sources of rational belief about reality. The brotherhood was open to anyone who took the moral faculties of man to be subject to necessary or constant general laws.

But the demands of *empirical* science soon placed constraints on what a Positivist might believe. Ethics, for instance, had to be naturalistic – utilitarian, perhaps, or evolutionary – so that its propositions could be more or less tested in experience. Then naturalistic ethics also became the casualty of a stricter idea of empirical science. The passage between 'is' and 'ought' became more hazardous, because mined by the naturalistic fallacy, until finally blocked later by the verification theory of meaning. Although the naturalistic fallacy has since been defused and the verification theory never stopped brave souls who believed in welfare economics or Skinnerian psychology, it is still canonical to distinguish sternly between positive and normative (and to warn sternly against confusing progress with change). Textbooks of social science still exclude normative propositions from rational scientific belief. Other casualties have been the organic, teleological and even mechanical concepts once commonplace in proposing natural laws. Darwinism, for instance, once a positivist key to the social world, has had to defend itself even as a proper biological theory of evolution. Malthus' iron laws of population, once a text book case of scientific detection, have become a lesson in the folly of going beyond all possible evidence. The father of positive sociology himself has been unmasked as a pedlar of speculations normative and metaphysical. Even Durkheim's *Rules*, the prayer book of orthodox methodology, contains much heresy if judged against *Language, Truth and Logic*.

What, then, does a strict positivist believe? Let us focus on the notion of experience which derives from Hume and

Hartley. The positive tradition gets its character from an insistence on the epistemic primacy of direct observation. The senses give us our sole direct acquaintance with the world, our only source of unvarnished news. They reveal only what is particular and present. Whatever is absent in space and time and whatever is general can be known only by inference. Inference to the absent or general is justified only if it can, in principle, be checked by the senses. Science requires an assumption of order and, strictly speaking, order is not presented to the senses. But it is thought defence enough against the sceptic, if the order assumed consists only in the sort of particulars and relations we can be acquainted with. Hence Hume analyses the crucial relation of cause and effect as holding between events $a$ and $b$ when (i) $a$ is contiguous with $b$, (ii) $a$ is prior to $b$, (iii) whenever $A$ (events like $a$) then $B$ (events like $b$) and, on another note, (iv) we are accustomed to associating $A$ and $B$.[4] The upshot is to make the statement of a causal law a legitimate conclusion of an inductive inference, and so, supposing a solution to the dire riddle of induction, within the scope of empirical knowledge. It is done by stripping the concept of a law of all ideas like production, force, purpose or necessity, which would take us beyond possible experience. That leaves the idea of correlation to do the work but, aided by a sophisticated theory of probability and statistics, it should be enough to wrest the empirical world from the Cartesian demon of doubt.

This meagre rendering is got by concentrating strictly on the epistemology of sense-experience. It gives no clue to the large battery of concepts used in Positivist philosophy of science or in the complex task of theory construction in works of Positive science. There is nothing meagre or simple about what is done in the application of Humean empiricism. None the less I judge that the root idea is very simple indeed. At the coal face, so to speak, very subtle methods are used for sorting true from false hypotheses about the world. Behind these methods are methodologies, issuing licences and criteria. Methodology is justified by principles defended in the philosophy of science, where complexity reaches a dizzying

---

[4] *A Treatise of Human Nature*, Book I part III.

order. But the philosophy of science is not autonomous and the theory of knowledge, in my view, provides the assay office of the last resort. Here I have in mind the delicate relation between ontology and validation mentioned earlier. Only theories which could be known to be true (or probably true) are worth passing up the line. Epistemologically, the criterion applied in the assay office of Positivism is that any theory must be testable. In asserting that, for Positive purposes, a natural law is basically of the form 'In conditions $C$, $A$ is a sufficient condition for $B$', I do not seek to quarrel with more elaborate formulations in the philosophy of science. For instance anyone concerned to tailor the basic idea to the range of causal explanations in legitimate use in science and everyday life may well prefer to define a cause as 'an *in*sufficient but *n*on-redundant part of an *u*nnecessary but *s*ufficient condition.'[5] There is no conflict, unless this definition requires a different theory of perception. Equally I pick no quarrel with Positivists, who include a notion of 'natural necessity' in their formula for a natural law, provided again that there are in principle empirical tests for natural necessity. The root idea remains, however, that $a$ caused $b$ if and only if in those conditions $A$ is a sufficient condition for $B$.

The root idea is enough to make sense of the text-book accounts of sound method offered to students of the social sciences. Fig. 5 (overleaf) is a clear and instructive example from the start of Walter Wallace's *Sociological Theory*.[6]

Its components are four stages linked by four methods in a clockwise process. In illustration Wallace uses the honoured example of suicide. We start, he says, by making 'direct observations on several persons who have committed suicide'(!). Having categorised the victims and computed rates by category, we can transform the observations into an empirical generalisation like 'Protestants have a higher suicide rate than

[5] J. L. Mackie, *The Cement of the Universe*, Oxford, 1974. Mackie holds the floor at present with his judicious and detailed version of what is still discernibly a Humean analysis. If it is improper to refer to him in a discussion of Positivism, my remarks should be read as addressed to formulations in the classic works of Nagel and Hempel.

[6] Heinemann, 1969. Another lucid illustration is the opening chapter of P. E. Lipsey, *Introduction to Positive Economics*, Harper and Row, 1972.

45

Catholics'. Moving clockwise to the top box by 'logical induction', we ask ourselves, 'of what can the suicide differential itself be taken as a special case?' Possible answers are couched in theoretic statements like 'Suicide varies inversely with the degree of social integration' and 'Acts of personal disorganisation vary inversely with the degree of social integration.'

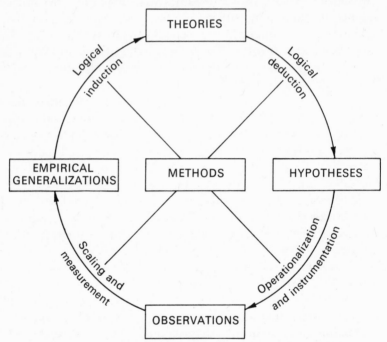

Fig. 5   *The components and process of scientific sociology*

Next, aided by suitable assumptions, we deduce further hypotheses, for instance that unmarried persons, being less socially integrated than marrieds, have a higher suicide rate. These hypotheses, operationalised, are tested by observation and incorporated into the next cycle, if upheld.

Simple though the diagram is, it presents a scientific factotum in miniature. There is a method of discovery (clockwise from Observations to Theories), a method of prediction (clockwise from Theories to Observations), a method of validation (repeated clockwise journeys) and a method of explana-

46

tion (anticlockwise from Observations to Theories). Wallace may be too optimistic as we shall see, but he nowhere breaks faith with a Humean epistemology.

For a rationale congenial to Logical Positivism, we cannot do better than consult Milton Friedman's distinguished essay, 'On the Methodology of Positive Economics'.[7] The task of a positive science, we learn there, 'is to provide a system of generalisations that can be used to make correct predictions about the consequences of any change in circumstances . . . by the development of a "theory" or "hypothesis" that yields valid and meaningful (i.e. not truistic) predictions about phenomena not yet observed'. A 'theory' is a blend of two distinct elements, 'a language' and 'a body of substantive hypotheses designed to abstract essential features of a complex reality'. In its former role 'theory has no substantive content; it is a set of tautologies. Its function is to act as a filing system.' In its latter role 'theory is to be judged by its predictive power for the class of phenomena which it is intended to explain'. The essay remains a storm centre because of its claim that the merit of a theory is independent of the realism of its assumptions. Also its later parts articulate a pragmatism at odds with the passages I have just cited. But these quotations catch perfectly the idea that scientific truth always lies with independent and objective facts, known by observation.

Putting Wallace and Friedman together, we can list several propositions typical of Positivism. A natural law is a regularity in nature holding in specifiable conditions; we know we have found one, when we have a well-enough confirmed theory; a theory is a set of logically-linked, high-order generalisations; the only test of a theory is the success of its predictions; prediction and explanation are two sides of the same and only coin, in that explaining a phenomenon is finding a theory from which it could have been predicted. Also, taking a hint from what is left unsaid, we can add that the same method holds for all sciences and that normative statements have no place in science.

---

[7] *Essays in Positive Economics*, University of Chicago Press, 1953, Chapter 1, pp. 4–8 in the Phoenix edition, 1966. For a discussion see M. Hollis and E. J. Nell, *Rational Economic Man*, Cambridge, 1975, Chapter 7, appendix.

How adequate is the basic idea that a natural law is a regularity holding in specifiable conditions? There are huge snags, so famous that the reader will again suspect an Aunt Sally. But the snags, although easy to see, are hard to remedy. It is perhaps unsporting to cite the hoary old Riddle of Induction, which besets all efforts to justify the underlying assumption that a regularity in the past is *pro tanto* good evidence that it will hold in the next case. I doubt if Wallace and Friedman are in any worse fix than other kinds of empiricist and I have no space to tackle the topic. It is worth pointing out, however, that the number of past cases is not necessarily the arbiter of merit for a theory. There are plenty of well-confirmed generalisations not usually regarded as natural laws. For instance in developed economies the capital–labour ratio appears to be about 3:1, the rate of profit about 12 per cent, the share of GNP going to labour about 40 per cent. An economist might be willing to bet on these constancies but he would be unlikely to regard them as natural laws. Confirmation is not to be treated in a flatly numerical way.

The general snag here is that correlation is not enough. Even granting that the past is evidence, we need to be able to tell a law-like generalisation from an accidental one. Otherwise nothing said so far is an adequate answer to the question 'How is science possible?' I shall assume that J. S. Mill is right when he says, 'It is not the empirical laws that count but the causal laws which explain them.' (*System of Logic*, Book VI, chapter 7.) He means that we can know that a generalisation is truly an empirical law, only when we have a causal law to explain it. The same thought is implicit in Wallace's diagram, when we have to advance to a proposition about degrees of social integration before accepting that Protestants do truly have a higher suicide rate than Catholics. But asserting the distinction is a far cry from justifying it and we must ask what a Positivist can think it a distinction between.

There are several replies which make good sense of scientific practice but have no warrant in Positivist epistemology. One possible virtue of explaining suicide rates through degrees of integration is the elegance and economy of the theory. But, whatever a Pragmatist would say, elegance and economy have no epistemic worth in Positivism. Another is its hint of the sort of reasons for suicide which a Protestant would be more likely than a Catholic to find cogent. This touches a main topic of later chapters but here and now it serves only to suggest further causal links. Since our problem is precisely that we do not see what is in principle sufficient to constitute a causal link, it is as yet no help to be directed to one kind of cause rather than another. Besides Positivism treats the sciences as all of a piece and there is nothing analogous in the natural sciences. A further possibility is that there is an *a priori* connection stemming from the (somewhat woolly) concept of integration. But, however tempting we shall find the idea presently, Friedman is certainly right to reject it on behalf of a Positivism, which denies explanatory value to analytic propositions belonging to the filing system.[8] Or again there is the mere fact that the higher level theory does succeed in removing some of the original puzzlement. But Positivists will protest (rightly, I submit) that unscientific or mistaken theories can also perform this service and that the psychology of puzzlement is no factor in epistemology. So it looks as if the only legitimate reply is that the higher level is more general and covers other groups too. But why, we retort, does this increase its claim to express a natural law?

To put the snag in another way, we have no epistemic reason to prefer the higher level to the lower. A theory is being treated as a set of logically-linked hypotheses, together with definitions, assumptions and transformation rules. Since truth always lies in independent, contingent facts, the only explanatory element is the hypotheses. Definitions contribute no truth; nor do assumptions, unless they are the established hypotheses of some other theory. For deductive inferences there are formal criteria of validity, which make the soundness of the inference a matter of the relation between premises and

---

[8] The most lucid summary and defence of a Logical Positivist theory of *a priori* knowledge is perhaps A. J. Ayer, *Language, Truth and Logic*, Chapter 4. As a sign of its influence in the social sciences, I quote P. A. Samuelson: 'It is clear that no *a priori* empirical truths can exist in any field. If a thing has *a priori* irrefutable truth, it must lack factual content. It must be regarded as a meaningless proposition in the technical sense of modern philosophy.' *Collected Scientific Papers*, ed. J. E. Stiglitz, MIT Press, 1966, Vol. II, paper No. 126, p. 1751.

conclusion and not of the truth of the premises. But the explanatory value of a scientific theory cannot be judged formally. Any observation statement or empirical generalisation can be presented as the implication of a higher level hypothesis. The ineradicable question is whether the higher level hypothesis is true. So far the question is no different in kind at higher level. It is merely harder, because the more general the hypothesis the less well confirmed it is likely to be.

It is open to Aunt Sally to cut her losses and declare that levels are simply conveniences in the exposition of theories. She could try rubbing along, epistemologically, without the usual distinctions between description and analysis, between realism and abstraction, between historical trends and theoretical connections. But such frugal reliance on induction alone would accord so ill with scientific habit and philosophic ambition that I shall not pursue the point.[9] From now on I shall assume explicitly that sound theories have some, so to speak, emergent property which makes them more than a set of empirical generalisations and that this feature bears on the problem of telling the lawlike from the unlawlike. We shall find the assumption as hard to justify as it is easy to make.

Although Wallace's diagram, relying on the acclaimed virtues of the Hypothetico-deductive method, invokes 'logical induction' and 'deduction', it does not in fact involve more than induction as a method of validation. 'Logical induction' is presumably a device for introducing unobservables and 'deduction' in effect a device for eliminating them. What validates theory is confirmation or, to put it formally, inferences of the form –

(1) if $T_1$ then $O_1$
(2) $O_1$
$\therefore$ (3) $T_1$ is confirmed.

Here $T_1$ can include factors, like the degree of social integration, which it would be hard to square with a method of discovery which relied solely on crude induction by simple enumeration of observables. But such factors are admissible, only if there is an indirect test for them in the success or failure

---

[9] *Rational Economic Man, op. cit.*, chapters 1–4 is less forbearing.

of the predictions they entail. There is a gain in sophistication for the construction of theories but a new snag in validating them. For, were the prediction derived by crude enumeration, we would at least know what hypothesis a successful prediction confirmed. With unobservables admitted, however, there are always infinitely many incompatible theories which all cover the known facts and all imply $O_1$. If whatever confirms $T_1$ also confirms $T_2$ which entails that $T_1$ is false, we seem to be in a pickle.

In Popperian eyes[10] the pickle is not serious, since there will, with one proviso, always be a further $O_2$ which is asserted by $T_1$ and denied by $T_2$. The proviso is that neither $T_1$ nor $T_2$ is the sort of theory which is consistent with all possible experience. Conveniently for the Open Society of liberals and pluralists, the proviso rules out the general theories of Marx and Freud and can be deemed to state the line of demarcation between science and pseudo-science. Whereas the inference above is invalid (except perhaps as a recursive definition of 'confirmation'), refutation uses the valid argument –

(1) if $T_1$ then $O_1$
(2) not $- O_1$
∴ (3) not $- T_1$.

It is falsifiability that counts, the genuinely scientific hypotheses being those which run a well-specified risk of refutation.

The effects of replacing confirmation by refutation are more than local. The one for us here is that science ceases to be directly cumulative, a progressive matching of discoveries to the actual fabric of the only world about us. Instead there are always infinitely many hypotheses unrefuted and infinitely many conjectures consistent with the known facts. There is still progress in knowledge but causal laws become, for purposes of science, the set of hypotheses we are at present willing to bet on. The riskier the bet, the higher the chance that we shall have to bet on a new set tomorrow and the greater the merit of survival. As Popper presented the idea in *Conjectures*

[10] Those still fixed on *Conjectures and Refutations*, London, 1969 and *The Logic of Scientific Discovery*, London, 1959. Popper himself seems to have changed ground somewhat in *Objective Knowledge*, Oxford, 1972.

*and Refutations*, it was a defence of the core of empiricism against misguided Positivist efforts to placate the Cartesian demon with a unique structure erected on determining truths of observation. Instead of tangling with the riddle of induction on the traditional frontier, he offered a criterion to distinguish science from pseudo-science.

It is idle to ask how this helps, unless falsification is free from the snags of confirmation. Alas, it is not. 'If $T_1$, then $O_1$; and not $- O_1$, so not $- T_1$' hides two crucial indeterminacies. One is that, since $T_1$ is a conjunction of several hypotheses, 'not $- O_1$' points the finger at no hypotheses in particular. We can stipulate which hypothesis is at stake. But it is only stipulation, in as much as we thereby assume that the others in $T_1$ are sound and there is no cogent reason to do so. Formally it looks as if we might pick out $H_1$ by finding two theories which both imply $O_1$ and differ only in that $H_1$ is asserted in one and denied in the other. But a theory is more than assortment and $H_1$ is part of the theory only if it is logically linked to other parts. Its isolation is therefore bound to be a contrivance which need not be accepted. The other, related, indeterminacy is that 'not $- O_1$' is itself a hypothesis. A commonplace of '-metrics' (econometrics, for instance) is that observed data have to be adjusted to get their true values and there is always room for dispute and reinterpretation. The values needed are those which would obtain, were external influences removed and measurement free from error. So a decisive test can be held only if the truth of some general statements is assumed. Whether a test has been repeated in the same conditions is partly a function of what the test shows. Here is one fairly precise sense in which there can be no theory-free facts.[11]

If these points are well taken, there is no aid to be had from Popper's vintage works and we must rethink Wallace's diagram. In effect there will be no rational bar to blaming the failure of prediction on the failure of ineliminable *ceteris paribus* conditions and so no way of showing science possible within traditional empiricism. The points cannot be proved at the drop of a hat and, if the reader can meet them, well and good.

[11] *Rational Economic Man*, chapters 1–4, puts a case with supporting arguments.

Doubting it, I shall leave him to try and invoke the weight of W. v. O. Quine to move us into the next phase. If empiricism must abandon belief in given, independent, objective facts as a crucial constraint on what it is rational to accept, what becomes of natural laws and causal explanation?

The temple of Positive science is giving us trouble partly because facts of observation are not as neutral as they need to be and partly because the distinction between matters of fact and the filing system stops us finding any epistemic value in higher levels of explanation. Quine attacks on both points. As it would be a sin to paraphrase him, I hope that a long and famous excerpt will be forgiven[12] –

The totality of our so-called knowledge or beliefs, from the most casual matters of geography and history to the profoundest laws of atomic physics or even pure mathematics and logic, is a man-made fabric which impinges on experience only along the edges. Or to change the figure, total science is like a field of force whose boundary conditions are experience. A conflict with experience at the periphery occasions readjustments in the interior of the field. Truth values have to be redistributed over some of our statements. Reevaluation of some statements entails reevaluation of others, because of their logical inter-connections – the logical laws being in turn simply certain further statements of the system, certain further elements of the field. Having reevaluated one statement we must reevaluate some others, which may be statements logically connected with the first or may be the statements of logical connections themselves. But the total field is so underdetermined by its boundary conditions, experience, that there is much latitude of choice as to what statements to reevaluate in the light of any single contrary experience. No particular experiences are linked with any particular statements in the interior of the field, except indirectly through considerations of equilibrium affecting the field as a whole.

If this view is right, it is misleading to speak of the empirical content of an individual statement – especially if it is a statement at all remote from the experiential periphery of the field. Furthermore it becomes folly to seek a boundary between synthetic statements,

12 'Two Dogmas of Empiricism' in *From a Logical Point of View*, Harvard, 1961, the 1st, 2nd and 4th paragraphs of section 6. Here and elsewhere I also have *Word and Object*, MIT Press, 1960, especially chapter 2, and *The Ways of Paradox*, New York, 1966, in mind. H. Putnam puts the ideas to striking use in 'Analytic–Synthetic', *Minnesota Studies in the Philosophy of Science*, vol. III. The clearest general case for a Conceptual Pragmatism, which I take to be broadly Quine's position, is still, in my view, C. I. Lewis, *Mind and the World Order*, 1929, Dover Books, 1956.

which hold contingently on experience, and analytic statements, which hold come what may. Any statement can be held true come what may, if we make drastic enough adjustments elsewhere in the system. Even a statement very close to the periphery can be held true in the face of recalcitrant experience by pleading hallucination or by amending certain statements of the kind called logical laws. Conversely, by the same token, no statement is immune to revision. Revision even of the logical law of the excluded middle has been proposed as a means of simplifying quantum mechanics; and what difference is there in principle between such a shift and the shift whereby Kepler superseded Ptolemy, or Einstein Newton, or Darwin Aristotle?

. . . . . .

As an empiricist I continue to think of the conceptual scheme of science as a tool, ultimately, for predicting future experience in the light of past experience. Physical objects are conceptually imported into the situation as convenient intermediaries – not by definition in terms of experience, but simply as irreducible posits comparable, epistemologically, to the gods of Homer. For my part I do, qua lay physicist, believe in physical objects and not in Homer's gods; and I consider it a scientific error to believe otherwise. But in point of epistemological footing the physical objects and the gods differ only in degree and not in kind. Both sorts of entities enter our conception only as cultural posits. The myth of physical objects is epistemologically superior to most in that it has proved more efficacious than other myths as a device for working a manageable structure into the flux of experience.

Any enthusiast for Paradigms will see at once where we are. Causal laws become general statements well-enough entrenched in our conceptual scheme to be above at least ready suspicion, when experience proves recalcitrant. They are aids in ordering experience and it takes something near a paradigm-shift to dislodge them. Wallace's circle no longer rests on a floor of fact but wheels freely in ways decided by elegance, economy and other criteria we could find no room for before. Pragmatism offers to make sound empiricist epistemology of such heady thoughts.

But careless talk costs lives, as the war-time posters said, and we cannot take the epistemological pretensions of Pragmatism on trust. It is all very proper to insist that our beliefs impinge on experience, must be revised when experience is recalcitrant and can be re-evaluated only at fixed prices. But it is most improper to let us always dispute the verdict or revise the tariff. More formally, the first order picture of testing is of a set of statements in fixed internal relations confronted by independent experience. The second order account of logical and other internal relations is that they too are revisable; and of experience that it is undiscriminated until interpreted within our conceptual scheme. The second order cancels the presuppositions of the first, leaving only a permission to do what we will. Admittedly *fac quid vis* is not automatically an invitation to chaos, since the will has its governors in our social system, habits of thought or, as Quine has since tried saying, in our biological constitution. In principle, however, an epistemology which rests science on experience interpreted at fixed prices must go on to justify at least one of these given constraints on rational belief. Pragmatist theories of truth and fact make both relative to criteria without objective standing.

Those who put faith in the sociology of knowledge will welcome the result. It is ironic that Pragmatism tries to correct Hume by making the mind active and ends by making it the creature of its own habits. It will amuse the gods of Homer to think of sociologists of knowledge using Quine's analysis of the web of belief as the first step in a structural explanation of its origin, maintenance and development. But I leave these ironies, together with the topic of paradigms, to a later chapter on the limits of intellectualism.

So far a bare notion of observable particulars has yielded too bare a notion of a natural law. We need Mill's distinction between the 'empirical laws' and the 'causal laws which explain them' but, epistemologically, cannot yet have it. Pragmatism, which lets us say what we want, does not stop us saying what we please. There is now a choice. We either enrich our ontology beyond what Positivism allows or strengthen the claim of theoretical connections to do what Pragmatism asks. There needs to be more to a natural law than regularity, if we are to tell the lawlike from the accidental, and the choice is whether to put the 'more' in the world or in the theory.

Looking to the world, we are inclined to think that causes *produce* effects. Friction generates heat, sparks make gunpowder explode, screams compel attention, poison brings

55

about the death of princes. Social facts, in Durkheim, constrain individuals, engender states of mind and embody forces. Everyday and scientific ontologies are so full of objects with powers that it may seem perverse to have delayed speaking of them so long. But, as Hume observes,

Should anyone pretend to define a cause by saying it is something productive of another, it is evident he would say nothing. For what does he mean by production? Can he give any definition of it, that will not be the same as that of causation? If he can, I desire that it may be produced. If he cannot, he here runs in a circle. (*Treatise* I. ii)

By a definition 'the same as that of causation' Hume means one arrived at with the same eye to the empiricist constraints, which account for his own definition. Production, as commonly conceived, is a process whose later states are brought about by powers and forces. A basic Humean empiricism rules out such powers and forces as beyond all possible experience.

If powers and forces are to be part of the world's furniture, the theory of perception must be adapted for them. Presumably they are not directly sensed but come in under the heading of unobservable entities, as aids to theoretical interpretation. They gain ontological standing because our best theories commit us to them. Hume's protest is heard at once. What kind of aid? What is best about our best theories? Why conceptualise experience in ways experience cannot confirm? Unless they break radically with his epistemology, believers in production will soon be running in a circle. Positivists cannot make the break and Pragmatists cannot yet justify it.

The objection, let me emphasise, is to injecting powers and forces into an empiricism derived from Hume. It does not dismiss the huge literature in the philosophy of science but does call for its epistemological licence. There may be other empiricisms; there are always rationalisms; and it might be argued that we no longer have to think in the terms of traditional epistemologies at all. I leave the topic open, partly from cowardice and lack of space, partly because the option of strengthening the claims of theory seems to me the more promising. But there are braver souls who undertake to enrich the world's furniture without abandoning objective criteria of validation and I cast no aspersions.[13]

As soon as natural laws are to be more than regular, the issue becomes not whether there is a necessity involved but of what sort. There are several to try for size at various epistemological prices. The clearest is the logical necessity attaching to truths of logic, mathematics and other formal systems and the clearest account of its relevance is the seventeenth-century one, which matched necessary truths to the only possible world. 'Nothing in the universe is contingent', wrote Spinoza (*Ethics*, I. prop. xxix) and worked out an entire supporting theory of knowledge. But I shall assume that a world where nothing is contingent is too high a price to pay for a clear notion of a natural law. We want a sense of necessity which leaves more than one course of history possible, something between a mere 'All $A$ are $B$' and the logician's '$\Box$ (All $A$ are $B$)'. The term in use is 'natural necessity', written '$\blacksquare$ (All $A$ are $B$)'. But the notation shows only that interest in such a notion is widespread. It remains everyone's problem to say what is signified by '$\blacksquare$'.

The strategic choice is whether to locate the necessity in the world and then to pick out the sort of theoretical statements which reflect it or whether to discern it in theoretical truths and argue from what is theoretically true of experience to what is therefore true in it. It might seem that there is little to choose, since the only way to justify an ontology is through epistemology and since every epistemology involves commitment to an ontology. But there will be a difference, I think, in the sense attaching to 'natural necessity'. To make the options clearer, it may be helpful to work with a fresh example. So let us recall Lionel Robbins' celebrated *Essay on the Nature and Significance of Economic Science*,[14] and his attempt there to explain the sense in which economic laws are 'necessities to which human action is subject'.

His *Essay* tries 'to make clear what it is that economists

---

[13]. See, for instance, R. Harré and E. J. Madden, *Causal Powers* or J. Mackie, *The Cement of the Universe*, Chapter 9 on 'pure laws of working'.
[14] Macmillan, 1932, second edition 1935, reprinted 1946. The editions diverge at important points, as we shall see.

discuss and what may legitimately be expected as a result of their discussions' (Preface), and he opens by defining economics as 'the science which studies human behaviour as a relationship between ends and scarce means with alternative uses' (p. 15). The kind of relationship he means is analytical or theoretical. He is not interested in a historicist approach, which would look for past trends in the allocation of scarce means. For, he believes, past trends (or empirical generalisations expressing what are alleged to be trends) are not to be relied on. 'However accurately they describe the past, there is no presumption that they will describe the future . . . there is no reason to suppose that their having been so in the past is the result of the operation of homogeneous causes, nor that their changes in the future will be due to the causes which have operated in the past.'[15] There are, in fact, two objections here, one to any mere inductivism, which treats causal laws as equivalent to trends discerned in past correlations, the other to a historicism which, while seeing the need to find causes of trends, treats the causes as homogeneous. Robbins hopes that his own analytical approach will deal with both objections. We share the hope, since it is idle to insist that there is more to a causal law than regularity, unless the 'more' also allows us in principle to detect causes which are not homogeneous. In other words Robbins sets himself what I have tried to show to be the right problem.

What, then, is a homogeneous cause and how do we know when we have found one? He gives two answers, each present in both editions but with different weighting. In the 1932 edition the initial definition of economics is made crucial, by way of a comparison with mechanics. 'In pure Mechanics we explore the implications of the existence of certain given properties of bodies. In pure Economics we examine the implication of the existence of scarce means with alternative uses' (p. 83 in both editions). 'Economic laws describe inevitable implications.' (1932, p. 110; 1935, p. 121) Without trying to be faithful to Robbins' intentions, let us ask what kind of implications. Are they implications of the definition of economics or

[15] 1932, p. 101. 1935, p. 109 is almost identical.

of the existence of scarce means? The latter alternative is tempting to anyone who thinks the world governed by forces but I cannot find a suitable sense of 'implication'. We do say that a poor harvest implies famine; but we mean either something which begs our question about natural necessity or something expressible in theoretical connections. Equally it is clearer to treat mechanics as a theory of the implications of certain given *statements* about the properties of bodies. In similar vein, we have L. von Mises' word for it that, 'In concept of money all the theorems of monetary economics are already implied.'[16] The effect is to trace the necessities to which human action is subject back to the axiomatic or definitional statements introducing the key concepts. That is not in itself contentious. But, whatever Robbins may have had in mind, we can make it contentious by suggesting that these are *real* definitions. A real definition purports to capture the essence of either the thing or the concept defined. I shall make space for this option presently.

The 1935 edition makes more of a 'necessity' which Robbins claims to discern in experience. Economic analysis is again treated as a set of linked statements but now it 'consists of a set of deductions from a series of postulates, the chief of which are almost universal facts of experience, present whenever human activity has an economic aspect' (1935, p. 99). These almost universal facts are known to us by an introspection which divides the social from the natural sciences. 'In Economics, as we have seen, the ultimate constituents of our fundamental generalisations are known to us by immediate acquaintance. In the natural sciences they are known inferentially.' (1935, p. 105) The three most basic postulates are that there is more than one factor of production, that we are not certain about future scarcities and that consumers have orders of preference. They 'do not need controlled experiment to establish their validity: they are so much the stuff of our everyday experience that they have only to be stated to be recognised as obvious . . . yet in fact it is on postulates of this sort that the complicated theorems of advanced analysis ulti-

---

[16] *Human Action*, William Hodge & Co., London, 1949, p. 38. See also his *Epistemological Problems of Economics*, Princeton, 1960.

mately depend.' (1935, p. 179) Here we have lawlike distinguished from unlawlike by making the genuine laws either known to us by acquaintance or deducible from statements of laws so known. Robbins has already pointed out blandly that 'if the premises relate to reality, the deduction from them must have a similar point of reference' (1935, p. 104). He is not the only thinker to try accounting for necessities found in theoretical statements by appealing to very general facts of experience.

In both editions Robbins speaks of needs, forces and market mechanisms but we should not treat these push-and-pull items as a third kind of necessity. If they could simply be asserted, he would not have had to write the book. He (rightly, I submit) treats them as metaphors to be cashed and justified. He also makes use of the purely logical necessities which relate axioms to theorems or relate premises to conclusions of arguments. But (again rightly) he does not suppose that the truth of his postulates has to do with the logic which relates them to their implications. Thirdly, although he claims a sort of psychological necessity for his postulates, he does not confuse psychological habit with epistemic conviction and makes no general attempt to explain causal laws in terms of a psychology of belief in them. Summing up, then, we can put aside physical, purely logical and psychological necessity and leave ourselves with definitional and experiential necessity as leading contenders.

I leave it to others to defend the claims of 'almost universal facts of experience' known by introspection. Nor am I competent to defend the Austrian school against economists who find Robbins' postulates not only less than evident but actually false.[17] The snag is to find an account of introspection which would allow knowledge of general truths. Perhaps some Cartesian would care to extend the clear and distinct perception of *cogito* to 'almost universal facts' but I cannot think an empiricist would tolerate general laws known by immediate acquaintance. Short of such heroics, we shall have to treat necessities in experience as problematic. Accordingly we

---

[17] See *Rational Economic Man* pp. 202f. and references cited there.

refuse Robbins' invitation to distinguish here between social and natural sciences and shall continue to look for a notion of causal explanation to apply across the board.

Defintional necessity, on the other hand, strikes me as more promising than is usually thought. The idea is to treat economic theory as a sort of social geometry, whose theorems derive from axiomatic truths of economic behaviour. Schematically, at any rate, we can set out the type of explanation by following up the comparison with mechanics. No doubt we were all asked in our schooldays to predict the fate of a foolish beetle ambling along a cylinder without noticing the slope of the ground. In less romantic words, an object moving laterally across a cylinder of given momentum will, *ceteris paribus*, be transferred from top to bottom of the rolling surface in a deducible manner. Given laws of mechanics, logic and mathematics and given direction, speed and other initial measurements, the student can tell just where the hapless insect will be crushed. He does it by applying a model which yields values for some variables, given the values of others. The general form of the exercise is –

$$M \rightarrow ((C \text{ and } ceteris \ paribus) \rightarrow (S \rightarrow R))$$

where '$M$' is a statement of the model

'$C$' is a statement of the 'stimulus' $(C_1, C_2, \ldots, C_n)$
'$S$' is a statement of the 'stimulus' $(S_1, S_2, \ldots, S_n)$
'$R$' is a statement of the 'response' $(R_1, R_2, \ldots, R_n)$
'$(S \rightarrow R)$' subsumes systematic functions of the form $(S_j \rightarrow R_j)$.

This form has several instructive uses, depending on which values are given and what questions are asked. It can be used to predict the value of $R$ for given values of $S$ and $C$, other things being equal. (The beetle will be crushed and 'X' marks the spot.) It can be used to explain a given value of $R$ by finding the values of $S$ and $C$ which, *ceteris paribus*, imply it. (The beetle was crushed at $X$ because it started from $Y$ etc., the connection being shown causal by invoking the laws of mechanics.) It can be used to produce a given value of $R$ by engineering a situation which brings $R$ about. (To kill a beetle at $X$, place it at $Y$ etc.) It is, in short, a convenient device for assembling all the predictive, explanatory, programming and productive roles of theory in mechanics, economics or any other science.

Epistemologically, however, we need more than a convenient device. Otherwise we have only a convenient way of restating all the previous problems. All depends on what we say about the statements of $M$. We would like to hold that theorems of the $(S \rightarrow R)$ form assert genuine connections because they are deducible from premises which include the statements in $M$. In plainer English, the idea is that connections are lawlike, only if they are derivable from, among other things, a sound theory. The idea helps, only if the statements in $M$ are true, without being either empirical generalisations or empty tautologies. Yet, granted what we have said about paradigms and underdetermination by experience, they are more like tautologies than generalisations. So, it seems to me, the most promising line is, in effect, to deny that tautologies need be empty and that is why there was mention earlier of real definitions.

The statements of $M$ are not tautologies, if a tautology is defined as a statement whose truth is guaranteed by logic alone. Although there is dispute about the exact scope of logic, it is safe to say that concepts like 'force', 'utility', 'scarcity', 'integration' are not concepts of logic. Any formal system with a domain (for instance neo-Classical micro-economics) includes concepts which mark its domain (for instance 'utility'). The concepts are essential both to the axioms and to the implications of the system. Let us recall von Mises' remark that, 'In the concept of money all the theorems of monetary economics are already implied.' Suppose, for purposes of argument, that monetary economics is self-contained, in the sense of having premises which introduce the concept of money without deriving it from elsewhere in economic theory. Then we have some axioms, $A_m$, some monetary theorems, $T_m$, and the relation between them, $A_m \rightarrow T_m$. The concept of money occurs essentially not only in $A_m$ but also in $T_m$ and in $A_m \rightarrow T_m$. In other words the relation between $A_m$ and $T_m$ is not purely one of logic, since, as far as logic alone is concerned, $A_m \rightarrow T_m$ is only contingent. To show that anyone asserting $A_m$ and denying $T_m$ would contradict himself, we must appeal to the concept of money occurring essentially in $A_m$. Moreover, to assert that $T_m$ is not only implied but also true, we must know that $A_m$ is true. What makes a formal system an economic theory is the essential presence of economic concepts throughout. What makes an economic theory true is that some of its axiomatic statements are unconditionally true.

If we are to use conceptual truths and conceptual relations as an account of the 'necessities to which human action is subject', we shall have to break with Logical Positivism over the status of *a priori* knowledge. As noted, Samuelson has regarded any proposition of pure economic theory as 'a meaningless proposition in the technical sense of modern philosophy'.[18] It would be too coarse to ask whether, in that case, he deserves a Nobel Prize for writing volumes of meaningless propositions and too curt to assume that Logical Positivism was just wrong about analytic truths. So we had best work in the subjunctive. *If* there were a theory of *a priori* knowledge which makes conceptual truths as objective a part of our knowledge as are truths of fact, then we could account for the missing difference between empirical laws and the causal laws which explain them. *If* there were, in Kantian spirit, unique ways of conceptualising domains of experience and it made sense to speak of getting it right, then theory would have an honest task of showing why what is must be. To explain a fact would be to find another to count as its cause, so that, when the facts were described in correct theoretical terms, the existence of the *explanandum* $(R)$ was deducible from a statement of the theory $(M)$, the conditions $(C)$, *ceteris paribus*, and *explanans* $(S)$.

It will be objected that, even if there were such a theory of *a priori* knowledge, it would not help, since all the original problems would arise in its application. How would we know that economic behaviour was essentially to do with scarcity (rather than, say, the conditions for production, exchange and reproduction)? How would we know which parts of economic activity fell under which economic concepts? It is all very well to build into the definition of 'sound theory' a

[18] *vid. sup.* p. 49.

guarantee that apparent counter-instances will have been mis-described but how does that help us distinguish good science from bad? In brief reply, I wish to distinguish between methodology, epistemology and ontology. Methodologi-cally, it can only be virtuous to leave scope for enquiry and experiment. The scope would be analogous to the testing of conjectures in mathematics. In the end, no doubt, we shall be able to prove or disprove Fermat's last theorem but, until then, we seek negative instances, offer partial proofs and find ways of showing it more or less likely that the propositions at issue are indeed necessarily true. It is in principle no more a threat to empirical science than to mathematics that the aim would be to arrive at necessities.

Epistemologically, there is now a contentious view of mathematics and of *a priori* knowledge to defend. To attempt it would need another book and I shall leave the matter in the subjunctive.[19] The root question is whether necessary truths can be shown importantly distinct from contingent truths (contrary to Pragmatism) without making them empirically vacuous (as Logical Positivists would suppose). Those who lack rationalist ambitions will prefer to settle for some other account of natural necessity. But there are also the epis-temological queries raised by trying to assimilate other sci-ences to mathematics. I do think that a single notion of causal-cum-theoretical explanation holds for all sciences but I shall later deny that it is the only notion required in the social sciences, where 'rational man' models will be given crucial scope. I do think that mathematics is the most promising ideal type for causal-cum-theoretical explanation but I do not thereby instruct psychologists to borrow their models from physics or sociologists from economics. The thesis is that action is always partly determined, in a sense which may (or may not) be best given by reference to geometry or mechanics, but need not be wholly determined. Epistemology is asked to treat the notion of a 'sound theory' within a theory of *a priori* knowledge but without destroying all distinction between

---

[19] Arthur Pap, *Semantics and Necessary Truth*, Yale, 1958, contains the arguments I would be most willing to rely on.

natural and social sciences and without forcing distinct sciences into an identical strait-jacket. This task too would require another book.

Ontologically we should decide how strong a kind of natural necessity belongs in the world. At first sight it looks very strong. Apparently, to theorise in terms of structures is to commit oneself to believing there are the corresponding structures in reality. When theory implies a tendency for all cases of a kind, it surely implies that there is an actual force operating in some. After all, what is the use of a theory of suicide, if not to express actual pressures on actual victims? But nothing said here has required this relation of correspondence. To borrow a later point, the rational agent does the rational thing and theory explains why; but there is no ontological sense in which he has to. Similarly, although the snooker ball has to move as it does, the necessity arises only because it features in the solution to a theoretical problem in mechanics. I fail to see that we must conjure real forces into existence. An *a priori* notion of natural necessity seems at first to involve a stronger ontological claim than does an empirical notion. In truth, however, I think it involves a weaker one. We can rest content with wholly contingent connections among the referents of concepts, among which there are necessary connections. Empirical notions of natural necessity are forced into bolder claims.

I had better confess openly that I do think there is an account of causal explanation to be had along these Kantian lines. But there is no space for the large job of working one out and I do not mean the chapter to depend on it. The point is that the regularities of the moral world need to be treated as more than regularities. They have to be expressions of a necessity of some sort, making it a matter for theory to classify phenomena and to tell genuine laws from spurious concomitants. That much I take to be common ground and the rest is an attempt to show that the problem thus set is not just an invitation to scepticism. The line I have sketched in subjunctives will seem no more plausible to many than an offer to square natural necessity with empiricism seems to me. Equally those who believe in a realism descended from Hegel will want something more ambitious still.[20] So be it. But there is also a partial agreement about causality, which is crucial for the rest of the book and I shall end the section on Plastic Man by emphasising it again.

We have had no reason to doubt that causal explanation is explanation by citing causal laws. Nor, whatever the exact analysis, have we doubted that their role is to show the particular as an instance of the general.[21] If $a$ is the cause of $b$, then it is so in as much as there is a connection between $A$ and $B$ in the relevant conditions. The direction of fit is from the general $A$, $B$ to the particular $a$, $b$ and accordingly, there is no warranted prediction or explanation, until we are entitled to assert the law. Otherwise there is no telling the genuine from the spurious or, to put it formally, the statements which warrant the assertion of subjunctive conditionals from those which do not. Passive conceptions of man all treat explanation in this way and, conversely, I have maintained, all theories which take the general as the ground of the particular yield a passive conception of man. Secondly, causal connections are transitive. If $a$ caused $b$, which caused $c$, which caused $d$, then, whatever the exact interpretation of the arrow, $A \to B$, $B \to C$, $C \to D$ in the relevant conditions and so $A \to D$. The cause of the cause of $b$ is the cause of $b$ and the effect of the effect of $b$ is its effect. If we do not accept this in everyday speech, the writing of history or courts of law, then either we should or there is something amiss with a passive conception of man. For, combining naturalism with determinism, we cannot escape holding that the actions of Plastic Man have their antecedents far in the past and that responsibility, in so far as it exists, is transmitted undiminished from the past, through present action to whatever other agents do in response. As with freedom before, we

---

[20] E.g. R. Bhaskar *A Realist Theory of Science*, Leeds Books, 1975 or R. Keat and J. Urry *Social Theory as Science*, Routledge, 1975.

[21] Be it said that others do doubt it, among them J. L. Mackie in *The Cement of the Universe*, H. L. A. Hart and A. M. Honore in *Causation and the Law*, London, 1959 and M. Hesse in *Models and Analogies in Science*, London, 1963 and *The Structure of Scientific Inference*, London, 1974. Certainly plain men, scientists and lawyers do often dispense with at least explicit reference to general laws. But the epistemological question is how far the logic of validation can follow them. Although I would have made much more of the matter in a longer book, my epistemological verdict would still have been that it cannot, for reasons already indicated.

can find analogues of everyday notions of responsibility and, once again, there are standard arguments to show that they can coexist with or even presuppose determinism. But they are analogues. Where there is no autonomy, the buck never stops.

# 4

# *Life's short comedy*

What is our life? The play of passion
Our mirth? The music of division:
Our mother's wombs the tiring-houses be,
Where we are dressed for life's short comedy.
The earth the stage; Heaven the spectator is,
Who sits and views whoso'er doth act amiss.
The graves which hide us from the scorching sun
Are like drawn curtains when the play is done.
Thus playing post we to our latest rest,
And then we die in earnest, not in jest.
                                    Sir Walter Raleigh

We are dressed in the womb for life's short comedy. Heaven,
the spectator, sees more of the play than we ever could.
Heaven sees both the man and the mask. Of course, Raleigh
may be wrong. It may be that, if the actor could remove his
last mask, there would be no face beneath. That, in a sense, was
the moral of a passive conception of man. For, while there
might (or might not) be *homo psychologicus* lurking behind
*homo sociologicus*, neither offered an individual self of Raleigh's
kind. There were analogues of everyday notions of self-
identity and free action but they were analogues none the less.
We come now to Autonomous Man and shall try to find him a
frame of reference in the thin space between the inexplicable
and the causally determined. It is the turn of the rational
subject self to take the stage.

Most of us look askance at versions of the Social Contract,
which explain social institutions as the (often unforeseen)
results of pacts among fully-fledged pre-social individuals,
already blessed with conscious goals and a language for plan-

ning how to achieve them. Even neo-Classical economics, which comes close in some ways, is careful to hedge itself with *ceteris paribus* clauses. Yet what I have just called everyday notions of self-identity and free action owe much to a classic social atomism. I do not think myself that enough space can be made for Autonomous Man, if we allow social facts so little importance in the analysis of human agency and so, before trying to understand the self, shall spend this chapter setting the social stage. Then we shall be ready to look for the actors. The individuals who interact are not prior to the stock of characters society provides; but neither are the characters identical with the actors, as will be argued in the next chapter. There we shall advance a notion of the actor's identity which is a delicate blend of 'private' self with social 'self'. Then in chapter 6 I shall keep my promise to offer a non-causal mode of explanation, in the name of autonomy.

What is our life? The play of action. Informally the earth is a stage, where actors play characters and we must seek the man in the mask. Formally the earth is a social context of positions and roles and we must see how nearly they explain action. It may be objected already that not everyone thinks role-theory central. Positions and roles define what are often called normative structures. On the passive side, normative structures are explained by some in terms of non-normative structures (like forces of production) and by others in terms of psychological laws. On the active side, they are often analysed in terms of shared meanings or negotiations. I do not deny it but, equally, I am not attempting a survey. The concept of role seems to me to pose an evergreen puzzle for anyone trying to understand action in a social context and to do so in a way just formal and ambitious enough to be suggestive. The 'dramaturgical analogy' makes a pretty starting point, with actors who belong to the world of producer and audience in symbiosis with characters who belong to the playwright's cast of *dramatis personae*. But our business is with what the analogy is meant to illumine, the actor in the play of his own life. Here the concept of role marks out a domain which lends itself both to passive and to active conceptions of man and sets problems for both.

I shall treat roles as sets of normative expectations attached to social positions or what F. H. Bradley called in better English the duties of a station.[1] Positions are the static and roles the dynamic aspect of a normative classification of social actors. This is not the only way to begin but I take the idea to be present also in the seemingly weaker definition of role as the active dimension of a social position, since there too it is activity sanctioned by norms which counts. Quartermasters, for instance, have typical ways of writing off equipment on the quiet but it is not part of at least their public role to do so. They are also wont to keep more items in the store than appear in the ledger and to use the surplus for the benefit of careless friends. Here there is a case for regarding such civility as part of the role but only in so far as quartermasters who play strictly by the book are liable to the censure (as opposed to the mere disgruntlement) of their friends. In other words a role may have more 'duties' than are publicly recognised but the presence of a 'duty' depends on breaches being open to 'moral' censure. (The quotation marks are there to discourage any easy inference from 'duty' to duty, but I shall drop them from here on, since I shall not be speaking of ethical duties.) Normative expectations need not be explicit, still less created by law, and they imply nothing about ethics, but they sanction social rules, prove their existence and, we shall find, are a source of reasons for action.

'Normative expectations' sound forbiddingly external and, so as not to start by making roles into a system over and against individuals, let us resume the image of the theatre, where actors are more intimately related to the characters they play. The dramaturgical analogy is a tempting one and the relation of actor to character seems simple enough at first. According to what we might call the Townswomen's Guild view, the actor dresses up for the occasion and pretends to be the character, the character is supplied by the playwright and the producer, as hidden impresario, sees that the pretence is faithful. But even this no-nonsense account yields conflicting ways of reading the analogy. On the one hand the actor, who

[1] F. H. Bradley, 'My Station and Its Duties' in his *Ethical Studies*, Oxford, 1876, reprinted 1962, chapter V. This and chapter VI are still wholly germane to our problem.

dons and doffs the mask, is wholly distinct from the *dramatis persona* and owes no part of his identity to the stage. Analogously, we might look to the extreme individualism which treats social life as a contract and a construct to be explained in terms of individual desires. On the other hand the script is complete, at least in traditional drama, and the character exists only in the play. Analogously, the actor is presumably in turn a character in the larger play of his own life. His identity is socially created and his behaviour is to be explained in terms of a programme he did not write. One analogy points to Autonomous Man, the other to Plastic Man.

Moreover both ways of reading the analogy contain further ambiguity. To separate actor from character is also one device for bringing *homo psychologicus* back into a passive conception. Conversely it need not threaten autonomy to see the actor as the character in his own life, if we insist that plays are not about characters (who exist only in the context of an audience) but about individuals. Even the existence of a playwright's script is none too sinister. At worst it poses the threat to free will, which some theologians have found and others denied, from an omniscient Creator, who knows already what I shall choose tomorrow; and it does so with a hint that even a divine playwright creates the play through the eyes of his characters. Besides, there are plays with deliberately incomplete scripts. Even with a stage set for amateur theatricals there is no such thing as the dramaturgical analogy, nor even the two dramaturgical analogies.

The plot thickens further as soon as theatre ceases to be seen as pretence. The mark of great acting is that the character lives in the actor and becomes part of his self-image. The actor does not so much impersonate the character as personify him.[2] We are now up against conflicting theories of the nature of acting. The phenomenon is opaque and, although some plays and performances put a clear interpretation on it, the interpretation can be disputed. Hence the true charm of the dramaturgical analogy is not to act as a measure but to pose the original

---

[2] I owe this point to Malcolm Bradbury. See M. Bradbury, B. Heading and M. Hollis, 'The Man and the Mask: A Discussion of Role Theory' in J. A. Jackson, ed., *Role*, Cambridge, 1971.

problem in all its suggestiveness. The fusion of 'private' self with social 'self' is no easier to grasp in the theatre than in everyday life.

The question pointed up by drama is whether roles create agents or agents create roles. For Plastic Man social facts and individual programming (in whatever proportions) must account for everything in the human scene. The positions and roles attached, who is inducted into them and how, styles of performance and the impact of sanctions, general requirements and individual embodiments are all matters determining the agent's identity. By all means include subjective and intersubjective meanings, provided they are derived from somewhere like a central value system by processes like socialisation and internalisation. The crucial point is that the playing of roles is always *explanandum* and never *explanans*. The notion of role is no doubt handy for picking out features of social life worth explaining but theoretically it is otiose, which is perhaps why it can often be deleted throughout works on role theory without loss of content. For Plastic Man it is only a metaphor that the earth is a stage.

For Autonomous Man the notion of role offers an *explanans*. Agents create their roles, or at least influence everything just cited as determinants of identity. But the claim should be worded cagily. It is all too easy to plunge for the ghostly individualism which makes men and women into abstract and absurd angels in a historical vacuum. Alliances then become dangerously confused. Bradley, for instance, is utterly scornful of the Individual. Working with a social-cum-organic theory of the agent's identity, he proclaims that 'there is nothing better than my station and its duties nor anything higher or more truly beautiful. It holds and will hold its own against the worship of the "individual", whatever form that may take.' 'My station,' he thunders, laughs at Individualism's 'adoration of star-gazing virgins with souls above their spheres.'[3] Well, so it does; and his Ethical Studies leaves the duties of stations weighing oppressively on their cowed incumbents. Also he makes social stations as immovable as

[3] *Loc. cit.* p. 201.

those on a railway system. But the famous essay is not his last word. In the very next chapter he presents an ideal of self-realisation beyond the duties of stations and the tenor of the book's metaphysic is towards an active conception of the social self. Taking allies where we find them, we make no individualist assumptions about the identity of the agents who are to create their roles. Provided a man can make his roles essential to being who he is and do so without losing his autonomy, we may yet have the best of an old argument. At any rate, Autonomous Man has a clear interest in a notion of role which is both a source of reasons for action and a vehicle giving him control of his own social life. That the earth is a stage is for him a categorial fact.

Role is *explanandum* in passive conceptions, *explanans* in active. There cannot be a continuum; over explanations of the last resort no compromise is possible. But, once this is granted, we must notice the problems as well as the advantages of making roles central to explaining social life. Plastic Man must budget for innovation, role-distance and other ways in which the script of the drama seems incomplete. Autonomous Man must keep a space for the self and star-gazing virgins need not despair. We note the limits as well as the scope of role theory in setting the social stage. None the less we have an idea to work with. It is that social action has what I shall call a normative explanation. In so far as

(1) the agent occupied a position with a role $R$ requiring action $A$

(2) the agent knew that $R$ required $A$

(3) the agent did $A$ because of (1) and (2)

we have the bones of an explanatory scheme. I hasten to add that it will be amended shortly but even so crude a version gives us a start.

With an abrupt change of discipline, although not of theme, I shall now borrow Quentin Skinner's analysis of an episode in eighteenth-century British politics, intended to make clear the relation of social and intellectual context to the conduct of a historical actor.[4] The topic is the persistent attacks by Boling-

---

[4] 'The Principles and Practice of Opposition: The Case of Bolingbroke versus Walpole' in N. Kendrick, ed., *Historical Perspectives: Studies in Thought and Society*,

broke on the ministry of Sir Robert Walpole in the 1730s and, in particular the importance which the historian should attach to the principles expressed by Bolingbroke in explaining himself. Although Skinner's notion of context is not congruent with mine of role, we shall I hope find the differences as instructive as the overlap.

Throughout the 1730s Walpole was harassed in parliament and out by Bolingbroke and his friends. Skinner asks himself not so much why Bolingbroke took up the cudgels at all but why he attacked Walpole in the precise way he did. The attack was directed at two main points, one being that Walpole's ministry had no business to retain a sizeable land force when Britain was no longer engaged in any major European war, and the other being that the ministry was too free with pensions and places for its supporters. Why were these the lines chosen? The question is not novel but other historians have raised it in the context of the more general one, why Bolingbroke attacked Walpole at all. Their answer to the general one has determined their answer to the other. Broadly, Bolingbroke has been taken by some to be an adventurer and by others to be a genuine patriot. Those who see him as an adventurer offer only a token explanation of the lines of attack, since an adventurer uses whatever lies to hand and these lines happened to be convenient. Those who see him as a patriot presume that he was especially incensed by the practices mentioned. Thus neither band of historians tackles Skinner's question in any depth.

Reflecting on this lacuna, Skinner discerns a crucial assumption at work. Both approaches to Bolingbroke assume that a man's professed principles enter into the explanation of his actions, only if he professes them sincerely. So, if Bolingbroke was an adventurer, his professed principles provide no explanation, while, if he was a patriot, they explain at face value.

London, 1974. Skinner's interpretation of Bolingbroke is self-confessedly contentious but I borrow it without apology to other historians who might wish to object, since it illustrates the philosophical point, whether it is correct or not. I also have much in mind his admirable essay 'Social Meaning and the Explanation of Social Action' in P. Laslett, W. G. Runciman and Q. Skinner, eds., *Philosophy, Politics and Society*, Fourth Series, Blackwell, 1972. I am, as usual, grateful to him for letting me pillage his ideas in this wholesale fashion.

The shared assumption, however, seems to Skinner to over-
look the importance of ideology, the fabric of thought and
debate in terms of which men profess their principles and try
to justify their actions. He therefore rejects the assumption, on
the ground that Bolingbroke's choice of lines of attack would
have been the same, whether he was sincere or not. In the
context of the time any opposition to the King's ministry was
likely to seem *ipso facto* treasonable. So Bolingbroke had to
appear as a patriot, one bent on defending the true liberties of
England. Conveniently his Whig opponents' own ideology
of constitutional liberty condemned especially the keeping of
mercenaries and the centralisation of powers. So Bolingbroke
could patriotically denounce a peacetime army as mercenaries
and the award of places and pensions to supporters as failure to
observe the separation of powers. Thus existing ideology and
his professed patriotic principles explain his specific actions
completely. He had found the only strategy likely to oust
Walpole without provoking a charge of treason. Yet the explanation is wholly silent about Bolingbroke's motives, thus
showing that professed principles can be explanatory, whether
sincerely held or not.

I offer no comment on the historical aspects of Skinner's
account, except to note that more is left unexplained by it than
Bolingbroke's actual motives. Why for instance did the attack
not command more support among those who shared the
ideology of the time? One may also wonder whether the same
approach can be extended to the general question of why
Bolingbroke attacked Walpole at all and, relatedly, what the
historian is to mean by 'motive' as distinct from professed
principles and reasons for action. (I air these queries not in
criticism but because they will matter presently.) But I do wish
to focus attention on the style of explanation Skinner uses,
since it promises to help us put the notion of role to work in aid
of an active conception of human autonomy.

When we ask how close role-analysis can come to explaining action, we find a similar line of thought. At first sight the
crux is whether the agent has internalised his roles and
accepted their duties as his duties. In that case and no other his
social positions would be the source of both reasons and

motives for the action to be explained. But, on reflection, there is more to it. An action $A$ has a normative explanation, we suggested, in so far as

(1) The agent occupied a position with a role $R$ requiring $A$
(2) The agent knew that $R$ required $A$
(3) The agent did $A$ because of (1) and (2).

It will be seen that the third clause is obscure and is doing too much work. The 'because' in it is ambiguous between reason and motive and fails to make clear the step from (1) and (2) to the doing of $A$. We can read it as asserting that (1) and (2) caused him to do $A$ in that he was so well socialised that he always acted on a normative syllogism with true premises. This makes (3) into a statement of motive, where motive is so defined as to suit a passive conception of man. But, alternatively, we can treat (1) and (2) as reasons for doing $A$ which apply to this particular agent and (3) as asserting that these reasons were his reasons. This reading leaves his motive enigmatic, the subject of a further and different enquiry. Skinner bids us take the latter course and later, when several difficulties have been overcome, we shall accept.

A single role rarely requires a unique course of action and, even when it does, there is often more than one way of discharging the duty. The chief of police can deny that he is supposed to use his scarce manpower in hunting down pornographers and, even if he is, he can often discharge the duty by bustling about sporadically to no great effect. In general a role, while requiring some actions and forbidding others, leaves a range of permitted options. Typically it permits $A$ or $B$ (or requires the disjunction ($A$ or $B$)) and forbids $C$, thus yielding an explanation of why $A$ rather than $C$ but not of why $A$ rather than $B$. Admittedly this is something. If we enquire ignorantly why Bolingbroke did not attack Walpole for incompetence, it is enlightening to learn that public figures had a patriotic duty to respect the crown's choice of ministers. But we shall understate the claims of role theory, if we confine explanation to the citing of a single role.

Adding this point to the need to distinguish reasons from motives, we can rewrite our normative schema –

(1) the agent occupied positions with roles $R_1, \ldots, R_j$, requiring $A$

(2) the agent knew that $R_1, \ldots, R_j$ required $A$

(3) conditions (1) and (2) were the agent's reason for doing $A$.

The idea is to introduce two kinds of calculation into the proposition that $R_1, \ldots, R_j$ required $A$. Firstly if $R_1$ requires $(A$ or $B$ or $C)$ and forbids $D$, while $R_2$ requires $(A$ or $D)$ and forbids $B$, then the agent with roles $R_1$ and $R_2$ must do $A$ to satisfy the requirements. We get a sort of role algebra to render the indeterminacy of each role determinate in combination. Secondly knowledge that $A$ is required may call for scientific reasoning. The Chancellor of the Exchequer, for instance, may have a broad duty to reduce unemployment but it may take months of work in the Treasury to find an $A$ which will actually have that result and without thwarting other aims he has an equal duty to pursue. That tightens the schema and increases its scope. The final condition, on the other hand, is now weakened. By specifying that (1) and (2) are his reasons, we withdraw any direct claim about his motives. Where an agent does the only action his set of roles permits for the reason that it is the only action, then we have a complete and powerful normative explanation. The interesting question is whether a complete normative explanation is also a complete explanation.

Before taking it further, there are objections to parry, some to the very idea of position and role, some to the claim that normative explanation is genuinely explanatory. The former are, I think, for sociologists and I am not trying to teach them their business. But we cannot pass on without a word. Skinner's account of Bolingbroke relies heavily on the ideological context of the time and the conduct analysed is certainly social action. Yet, although it is crucial that Bolingbroke had to be seen as a patriot, it is far from clear that patriot is either a position or a role. Loosely, no doubt, we can speak of his patriotic duty and attach it to any of several positions, for instance that of member of parliament. But everyone else, including the government, had a patriotic duty too, whereas only Bolingbroke's supporters saw fit to attack Walpole for keeping mercenaries and upsetting the separation of powers. In general it is a nice problem for role theorists to say what positions there are in a society at a time or what roles with what duties attach to them. Are there nowadays roles of cyclist, drug-pusher, television personality or Englishman? Well, cyclists must keep off footpaths, pushers are sanctioned by clients if they peddle quinine as heroin, television personalities are *eo ipso* proper persons to launch supermarkets and England expects every man to do his duty this day. But it rings false to infer that drug-pusher is therefore a position with a role or a role attached to some other position. Equally a clear position may have critically unclear duties. When is a minister who deceives parliament bound to resign? Is an Anglican priest required to believe in God? Is a professor forbidden to seduce his own students?

An ambitious role theorist will reply that these are practical snags and blurs in a basically clear picture. But the trouble seems to go deeper. Position and role stand together as static and dynamic aspects of the same elementary form. Yet such clarity as the criteria for each have depends on an assumption about the other. It is explanatory to cite the fact that a man is an MP in so far as there are thereby normative expectations; which expectations are normative depends on whether theory is interested in what is expected actually, legally or morally; which option is theoretically best depends on which social positions it is explanatory to cite. Hence it seems that the ideological context from which Bolingbroke's reasons for action derive is prior to and broader than the dynamics of eighteenth-century social positions. The role theorist would like to reply by producing the missing criteria for settling the questions raised in the last paragraph. Since he cannot do so at present, he has to fall back on a promise. The reader will no doubt be able to decide whether to be content with a promise. For my part, I wish the role theorist success, since the idea of an ideological context seems to me too vague to rest with and role theory offers at least a promising way of making it precise. At any rate it is not in the philosopher's role to provide a definitive social map and I leave the issue with the thought that normative explanations do sometimes have clear and true premises. In any event the concept of role has served to raise our own problems.

The objection that normative explanation is not explanatory strikes nearer home. The first premise, that the agent occupies positions with $R_1, \ldots, R_j$ requiring $A$, holds usefully only if the agent has a consistent set of roles. Otherwise it holds vacuously, in the sense that an inconsistent $R_1, \ldots, R_j$ require $A$ but also require *not-A*. A set including $R_1$ which requires $A$ and $R_2$ which requires *not-A* (or requires $B$ which excludes $A$) cannot explain the doing of either. Role conflict being endemic, we can be charged with backing a sure loser. In reply, the charge can be rebutted by pointing to sorting devices like immediacy, hierarchy and severity of sanctions. Role conflict is only apparent where there are rules of priority. People do decide whether to betray their country or their friend and without abandoning either role. But rebuttal is not wholly convincing and an implied view of human nature which had men always behaving consistently within consistently ordered role-sets would strike most of us as fanciful. It seems wiser to recognise some limit to the scope of normative explanation, while also allowing for some internal ordering. The limit can either be descriptive or, so to speak, prescriptive. In other words we can grant that not all socially significant action does have a normative explanation and then treat the fact either as an invitation to add to the list of elementary forms or as a clue to the art of increasing human autonomy. The distinction will become clearer presently but, in either case, normative explanation still has a scope and, I shall maintain, a crucial one.

Objections continue with the second premise that the agent has to *know* what his roles do commit him to. This makes the schema apply wholly only to agents who are wholly socialised or wholly rational. That seems to exclude most of mankind. I grant the point but deny that it is an objection. The idea is to set up two ideal types of agent whose conduct has a normative explanation and then to explain departures in part by their degree of approximation. The two types will belong one to passive and the other to active conceptions. A highly socialised agent certainly knows and does what is expected of him. *De tautologis non disputandum.* But, by the same token, normative explanation within a passive conception is a mere first step in explaining how obedience to norms is produced and sustained. Highly rational agents, on the other hand, stand in a different relation to the norms which supply them with their reasons. It will be argued later that that is why the second premise is initially so strong. Until then it is enough that agents have a working knowledge of the next thing to do and I see no reason to suppose otherwise.

Let us grant, then, that agents do often have consistent positions and roles, which require a unique course of action, and, recognising what is required, do it. The objector now doubts whether or how far such citing of context explains. The doubt would be easily answered, had we made knowledge of the requirements into the actor's motive. Thus, to oversimplify, if Bolingbroke really was a patriot, one bent on doing his patriotic duty as he saw it, then we can indeed argue that what he did consistently with his professed principles he did because of his professed principles. That would leave some large questions for further scrutiny – was he truly a patriot? have we understood his social context? is there so direct a causal connection between context and correspondingly motivated action? But the strategy would be clear in principle, on the assumption that actors are creatures of social context and of given motives (which may or may not turn out to be the product of context too). Conversely, however, such an explanation would lapse if Bolingbroke turned out not to be a patriot and the notion of reasons was injected, so that the explanation could stand whatever the actor's motive. Granted that Bolingbroke could and did cite reasons for acting as he did, how can we know that these reasons were his reasons, in particular, can we know it without appeal to motives?

The cap fits but was the actor wearing it? As a general problem about the scope of normative explanation, it depends on what we assert about human nature. We have already noted that *homo sociologicus* is certainly wearing the cap which fits. Quentin Skinner's assumption, however, is more refined. It is to the effect that, in recognising good reasons for action which apply to him, the actor makes those reasons his own. The idea is to distance the actor from his context without thereby destroying the claim of context to explain action and the critic will doubt whether it can be done. Similarly, the very concept of role-distance seems to imply that the actor's real reasons are not those supplied by his roles. A dangerous dualism now threatens. On the one hand we have a public stage, constituted by positions and roles (and whatever there is in the embracing 'ideological context' which cannot be translated into role theory). On the other hand we have a hidden world behind the scenes where the real actor lives his real life. In the privacy of this mental sanctum, he engages in real relations with phantoms of the actors in the public drama. He alone has access.

It is a very dangerous dualism, not to be put aside as entailed but irrelevant. What makes the reasons in the role into the actor's own reasons is that the actor had a motive for doing his duty. Why I want to go to London may indeed have nothing to do with why I go by train rather than by car. But this is so only if I have a suitable motive for going to London. To get to a death bed I shall take the faster route; to attend a railwaymen's annual conference I may do well to arrive by train. So far the case of Bolingbroke shows only that reasons for choice of means may sometimes be distinct from motives for pursuing goals. Two questions have been distinguished where some historians have presumed only one. But their relation is not yet clear and, if it turns out that motives are always inaccessible, we are in trouble. If, moreover, we also find that we have avoided motives by a notion of distance which makes historical actors into egoists armed with linear programming techniques, the trouble will be fatal.

The simplest retort is that it is not my motives for going to London which matter but my reasons. Whether Bolingbroke was a patriot or an adventurer is a question about his reasons for attacking Walpole (as distinct from his reasons for mounting the attack in one way rather than another). So, if asked why Bolingbroke attacked Walpole at all, we can reply in the same sort of way as before, by finding a further goal in pursuit of which legitimating reasons for the attack were convenient. But this would either merely postpone the problem or solve it by losing the actor. Legitimating reasons will never help us decide whether Bolingbroke was a patriot or an adventurer, given that there was, within that context, no legitimate way of professing oneself an adventurer. So either the gap between professed and real reasons remains or it is closed by finding some part of the public drama which could not have been played with distance. The former option sounds attractive. By siting the actors on an indefinite means–end continuum, we can treat all their actions as *zweckrational* in their ideological context, without ever bumping up against an end which is not in turn a means. But there are two insuperable snags. One is that *Zweckrationalität* cannot stand on its own, since means are rational, only if ends are rational. This needs a long argument, which I shall attempt in chapter 6 and I mention it here only to give warning. The other is that we cannot afford to make questions about motives unanswerable.

Motives have been shabbily treated so far. They have featured as the crude drives and urges of a mechanical *homo psychologicus* within a very passive conception of man. It goes without saying that psychologists have far more interesting theories than that. So it is no objection to wondering whether Bolingbroke was an adventurer or a patriot that ambition and patriotism are not urges. But nor is it inevitable that, in speaking of motives, we pull the bolt on the trapdoor which drops the actor from the stage into the unconscious. Our concern with motives is an eclectic one and we do not have to decide among competing psychologies nor need we settle the boundary between psychology and sociology. Motive, for our purposes, is a desire defined in terms of its object. We need to find motives in order to fit the cap to the actor's head, where our notions of role and legitimating reason have so far only fitted his head to the cap.

That is why we have to go carefully with a hidden world behind the scenes (or beneath the floor). Autonomous Man needs distance and hence a gap between accounting for himself and accounting to himself. But the gap cannot be impassable. I do not quite mean that we must solve the Other Minds problem. I mean that we must be able to pose it. No doubt there is always room for argument whether we have identified a man's motives, indeed whether he had identified them himself. But there can be no argument until there are possible answers to a clear question. We must neither reproduce the social stage *in camera*, with all the original problems, for the benefit of just one participant observer; nor confine the furniture of the hidden world to items irrelevant to what passes on the social stage.

In terms of actor and character, then, we still deny that the actor's motives are the character's reasons, since the character has reasons supplied by the play without reference to matters off stage. Nor do we accept that the character's reasons are the actor's motives, since this, although holding for a passive *homo sociologicus*, leaves no room for autonomy. Hence, although no doubt we shall not wish to confuse Bolingbroke's motives for attacking Walpole with his reasons for accusing him of keeping mercenaries, we cannot leave it at that. It is some help to say that his motive for the accusation was his reason for the attack but there are still loose ends. Let us see what they are, in readiness for the next two chapters.

Autonomous Man takes the social stage as a character and so is the subject of two sorts of consideration. As character he has a role and duties or, if you prefer, the responsibilities assigned to the character. These duties involve norms rather than ethics and, as with the example of the Chancellor, science may be needed to work out how to discharge them. The result is a set of legitimating reasons for trying to achieve proper ends. But he is distinct from the character and the legitimating reasons are not automatically his reasons. To be precise, they are his reasons for the choice of means, granted that he has reason or motive to achieve the character's proper end. Presuming that role theory could cover the ground (or at least typifies whatever would), we have a normative explanation showing that the agent has a sufficient reason for doing $A$, a sufficient reason which was also his reason. So far so good. But Skinner's Bolingbroke has turned out too much of a special case, being one where doubt about the actor's own objectives did not infect our understanding of his choice of means. It is not true in general that there is only one legitimate means to an end nor that, without specifying the reason for seeking the end, we can say which is the best legitimate means. The actor wishes on the character the legitimate means which best suits the actor and we therefore cannot spin a general thesis from the case of Bolingbroke, while there is an impassible gap between professed reasons and real reasons. In the next chapter I shall try to close it by arguing that there are no criteria for the agent's identity, if all roles are played without commitment. In chapter 6 I shall try to justify treating 'real reasons' as the key, despite the fuss we have just been making about the relevance of motives.

At any rate we have set the stage for both active and passive conceptions. We have done it with the ideas of normative requirement and legitimating reason, construed formally with the aid of roles attached to social positions. Consequently it is an idealist stage, one where positions, roles, duties and actions are essentially meaningful. I take it that this suits all forms of actionism. The break between weak and strong comes over the scope of normative explanation. Both regard it as incomplete but on different grounds. Weak actionism takes the actor to be plastic and his actions to be caused by the normative structures requiring them. (There may be a non-contingent tie between norm and action, as we shall see in chapter 6, but there is also a causal relation.) Reasons, codified in roles, are motives for those required to act on them. There is such a phenomenon as role-distance but it is either built into the role or results from the presence of other roles. Normative explanation is complete as far as it goes but cannot explain why the system of positions and roles is as it is. It yields the cause of the action but complete explanation calls for the cause of the cause. Strong actionism, on the other hand, conceives the relation of action to norm on the assumption that men are (potentially) autonomous. Reasons codified in roles are legitimating reasons but they move the actor only when they are also his real reasons. Role-distance is distance of self from role. Normative explanation, instead of being a full first step in a two step explanation, is half an answer to the only question. In strong actionist eyes the actors are as responsible for the context as they are for deciding what to do in it.

Star-gazing virgins were earlier bidden not to despair and the last paragraph indeed gives individualism a free hand. It leaves the individual seemingly able to choose his roles, to propose interpretations of them once chosen, to invent new roles altogether. What he cannot do single-handed he can do with others, renegotiating by collective action what looks uncommonly like the Social Contract. If he finds social facts external and constraining, then he is duped, weaked-willed, unskilful or in bad faith. There is as much room for a self as you please. But this does not mean that I have been setting the social stage for the benefit of individualism. Like Bradley, I judge that the self needs to be social. Although a passive conception absorbs the actors into the characters, an active one need not make the characters mere masks. So far we have a passive mode which dispenses with the self and an active one which says almost nothing about it. But at least we have an approach to social interaction which would suit Autonomous Man nicely. We have the stage. Now let us look for the actor.

# 5

## Personal identity and social identity

I well recall having my identity tested in California fifteen years ago. Candidates were faced with a sheet of lined foolscap paper, topped with the single question 'Who am I?'. They had to respond with whatever truths about themselves they thought important, broadly either descriptions of their inner being or lists of their significant roles. Those who failed were deemed to have an identity crisis and hauled off to wooden shacks behind the library, where psychiatrists lay in wait with ink blots. Or so rumour had it, but I cannot vouch for its truth, as I did not stay the course. Having been nurtured in arctic regions of English society, where upper lips are stiff and chins up, the whole show seemed dreadfully bad form. Having been polished off on Oxford analytical philosophy, it appeared incomprehensible. At any rate, I wrote my name and then could think of nothing to add. Even that was a mistake, as the test was meant to be anonymous, but my name did strike me as a necessary and sufficient answer to 'Who am I?' Any other response, I reasoned, would be addressed to the different question, 'What am I?', thus, from a logical standpoint, confusing accidents with essence and, from a British point of view, confounding moral identity with social relations.

I was being absurdly insular and richly deserved the ink blots. A crisis of identity is more than a failure of confidence, displays more than what the army dubs 'lack of moral fibre' and cannot be dismissed in the Oxford idiom of the time as 'logically odd'. I give my name when postmen or dentists ask who I am but it will hardly do as an answer to myself. Conversely, knowing my own name is hardly a sufficient prophylactic, even in a primitive society like Britain where

87

names still have a ritual magic. Yet I remain puzzled by the question set. I am not in doubt that identity crises are real; but I do wonder what they are crises of. As a student of philosophy, I wonder why discussions of personal identity supply nothing which could be *en crise*; as a student of the moral sciences, I am still seeking a cogent account of the man behind the mask. In this chapter we shall try to find the missing actors for the characters on the social stage in our actionist drama by tying the strange lacuna in role theory to the philosophical problem of personal identity.

The strange lacuna is the one just where we hope to learn who plays the roles. Admirers of Erving Goffman, for instance, are well served with nuanced, coolly sardonic tales of how actors in the life-world play their parts with varying styles and skill, at varying degrees of distance and for varying ends. Interactions are far from mechanical and the actor can keep control of them by means of secondary adjustments, distancing rituals and elusive negotiations. If he succeeds, he has an identity not merely defined for him or thrust upon him; and this identity is crucial in understanding and explaining his conduct. Although 'identity' here is in part a set of attributes, it refers also to a subject or substance who manipulates his attributes and his *Umwelt*. Hence Goffman owes us a theory of self as subject, something more robust than a notional we-know-not-what, to sustain the active base for its social transactions. Notoriously the debt goes unpaid. There are some gestures towards self, for example 'a self is a repertoire of behaviour appropriate to a different set of contingencies',[1] 'by "personal identity" I mean the unique organic continuity imputed to each individual, this established through distinguishing marks such as name and appearance',[2] 'the self is the code that makes sense out of almost all the individual's activities and provides a basis for organising them'.[3] But, however pretty, such apothegms only tease. Were Goffman's actors simply creatures of their *Umwelt*, it might be enough to speak of repertoires, codes and organic continuity. But, for all

[1] *The Presentation of Self in Everyday Life*, New York, Doubleday, 1959.
[2] *Relations in Public*, Penguin, 1971, chapter 5, p. 189.
[3] *Ibid.* Appendix p. 366.

his fish-eyed, dead-pan glimpses of hidden rules and rituals, he has a foot in the strong actionist camp. His actors can and often do construct and control. Here repertoires and codes are not enough. What makes behaviour appropriate and decodes activities is precisely the identity of the actor which the notions of repertoire and code are perversely being used to define. Nor can organic continuity be what unifies the repertoire or holds the key to the code; and 'personal identity' (especially in scare quotes) cannot be something imputed, if it is a crucial *explanans*. There must be more to it.[4]

It is not obvious that those wanting a creative, autonomous self to fill the gap in role theory should turn to philosophical discussions of personal identity. Indeed it may seem irrelevant to do so. At first sight philosophers and sociologists use wholly different senses of 'identity'. The former typically seek logical and epistemological criteria by which persons can be identified and reidentified. The latter typically look for a theory of personality which will fuse psychology with normative structuralism. It would be a poor pun to say that both are concerned with relations of identity, when logical relations like symmetry belong in a different universe of discourse from social relations like role-partnership. An initial hope that both share an interest in the self-identity of persons is given pause on the philosopher's side by consulting the *International Encyclopedia of the Social Sciences*, where Mazafar Sherif has this to say in the entry for Self-Concept' –

Self is a developmental formation in the psychological make-up of the individual, consisting of interrelated attitudes that the individual has acquired in relation to his own body and its parts, to his capacities and to objects, persons, family groups, social values, goals, and institutions, which define and regulate his relatedness to them in concrete situations and activities.

To prove that it is not just the gruelling prose which stops the philosopher emulating Oliver Twist, here is a similar thought from Nigel Dennis' delicious novel *Cards of Identity*. It is a

---

[4] He has told me that he regards the issue as one of what frame of reference is best adopted for what purpose. In micro-sociology he recommends assuming free will, however untenable the assumption within wider frames. This is a neat way to parry realist questions but not one which seems to me to evade the need for a theory of the self as subject.

report by the bogus Captain Mallet of how he has just acquired a butler by brainwashing an unwary visitor to his stately home. It was easy work, he explains, but fatiguing –

It was having to sit up so late with him that tired me. And, as always, it was only when the last nail had been driven home that I realised how much my arm ached. His character was not strong, but he had been using it for a long time. It was quite rusted onto him. Why he wanted this identity so much, I cannot imagine. It was two a.m. before I convinced him that it was entirely his own invention.

I hope you have supplied him with a rich, full past [said Mrs Mallet]. Everything a respectable steward could want. As a lad, I decided, he ran away to sea. Twenty years of drink and women followed in all parts of the world. Now at last he is going straight and though we cannot *quite* assure him that he will ever atone for his sins we can at least assure him that he is no longer trying to escape reality.

The philosopher smiles but shakes his head. *Cards of Identity* is not about identity, he says.

Yet is it not? Philosophers' stock questions sound as if addressed to the same topics. What is a person? What differentiates one person from another? What unites different states of the same person? These are enquiries into identity of some kind. They invite criteria to individuate, identify and reidentify persons, conceived as particular members of a problematic sort. Social scientists do not use this language but they share an interest in the terrain. At least I shall try to show that they do by suggesting, firstly, that philosophers cannot solve their philosophical puzzles without an excursion into social theory and, secondly, that strong actionism falls, unless the actor is so conceived as to satisfy what philosophers call strict or numerical criteria for personal identity. These are criteria which not only are not but also cannot be satisfied by more than one candidate, a distinction which will become plainer presently. The terrain is hard and I offer no advanced guide to it.[5] The aim is solely to pick out places of interdisciplinary interest and, when I come to borrow William James' famous survey, it

---

[5] The large philosophical literature is rich in subtle and precise argument. See, for instance, B. Williams, *Problems of the Self*, Cambridge, 1973 or D. Wiggins, 'Locke, Butler and the Stream of Consciousness: and Men as a Natural Kind', *Philosophy*, 1976.

will be merely as a gross pointer to problems which still beset the subtlest discussion. Even on these terms the chapter will seem superficial and its conclusions are at best tentative. But I think the issues too absorbing and important to shirk.

If the old problems of personal identity remain enigmatic, it is partly because answers still have to pass old, severe tests, subject to Cartesian tests of demon-proof certitude. What is a person? Traditionally the question calls for *essential* attributes, necessary and sufficient to distinguish all persons from all other beings. So, however sure we are for example that all persons are in fact embodied in a single continuous body, a man cannot *be* his body, if he could possibly do without it. Whether he could depends for instance on whether Protestants have a coherent idea of a disembodied after-life and whether those science fiction stories of bodily interchange make sense. A huge snag arises at once. The relevent notion of possibility is not just that of logical possibility. It has to be the wider one of conceptual possibility and we have no cogent, or at any rate uncontentious, theory of conceptual possibility. Hence, even if the concept of a person is plausibly shown primitive in relation to those of body and experience in our conceptual scheme,[6] that helps us only if we know how to price a necessity of our conceptual scheme. Does such a necessity just happen to be part of the massive central core of Western thought or is it the sign of an eternal verity for any true concept of a person? What sort of error is made by those who disagree and can we be sure that they are indeed in error? Until we can answer, even Cartesian dualism, lately the butt of massive onslaughts, remains within the bounds of some sort of possibility. While essential attributes and logical guarantees are demanded, it remains proper to work with a broad canvas.

So let us recall William James' chapter on the self,[7] a text read by both social psychologists and philosophers. There James seeks 'a basic principle of personal unity' and dismisses what are still crudely the main three lines of thought. The oldest is that each of us is an enduring substance, keeping its identity through the series of our states of consciousness and

---

[6] vid. P. F. Strawson, *Individuals*, London, Methuen, 1959.
[7] *The Principles of Psychology*, 1890, Dover Books, 1950, chapter X.

physique but 'to say that phenomena inhere in a Substance is only to record one's protest against the notion that the bare existence of phenomena is the total truth' (p. 346). And James does record his protest, with a telling rebuttal of Humean, associationist attempts to treat the self as a bundle of self-adhesive, perceptual atoms. That leaves transcendentalism, deriving from Kant's offer to show the unity of the judging mind as a synthetic *a priori* truth in the ordering of experience. James gives him credit for recognising and stating the problem but none at all for solving it.

James' reckoning is no doubt too brief but, even now I submit, there are no leading texts which prove it clearly too harsh. Notions of substance and essence have revived in complex and promising forms but the puzzles have only deepened. Similarly we can still wonder what unites different states of the same person. It seems important that each of us has memories of his own past but logic does not forbid two persons to have the same memories or guarantee that anyone remembers enough to individuate him. On the other hand bodily continuity, despite a guarantee that two persons cannot be in the same place at the same time, is usually thought insufficient, since *personal* continuity needs more than the continuity of a physical parcel. Indeed it is bound to be insufficient, while, even on an hypothesis that persons are bodies, we cannot specify the predicates which would distinguish persons from other bodies.

These tendentious remarks are no substitute for reading the literature but, if they are at all fair, there is also a strange lacuna in philosophical discussion of personal identity. Baffled on other fronts, the philosopher might at least dally with a social dimension. Consciousness does not, even could not, operate in a vacuum and bodies are just bodies unless relations among them are endowed with shared meaning. It is not as if the thought is new to philosophy. James made much of it in the famous chapter in the *Principles* and the corresponding chapter in his *Psychology* (*Briefer Course*).[8] There he divides his attention between '(*A*) the self as known, or the *me*, the "empirical

---

[8] References which follow are to chapter 12 of the *Briefer Course* in the Collier Books edition of 1962.

ego" as it is sometimes called' and '(B) the self as knower, or the I, the "pure ego" of certain authors'. 'A man's Me is the sum total of all that he CAN call his, not only his body and his psychic powers but his clothes, his house, his wife and children, his ancestors and friends, his reputation and works, his lands and horses, and yacht and bank-account. All these things give him the same emotions.' (p. 190, his italics) The constituents of this (horridly bürgerlich) Me divide into the material me, the social me and the spiritual me. The bodily me centres on the body and extends through clothes, parents, wife and babes and home to all my property. A man's social me is the recognition he gets from his mates. 'Properly speaking, a man has as many social selves as there are individuals who recognise him' but 'we may practically say that he has as many social selves as there are distinct groups of persons about whose opinion he cares' (p. 192, his italics). The spiritual me denotes 'the entire collection of my states of consciousness'. 'The very core and nucleus of our self, as we know it, the very sanctuary of our life, is the sense of activity which certain inner states possess.' (p. 194) The Briefer Course says no more but the Principles continues with a matchless description of James' own self-consciousness, the most intimate aspect of which is found to consist mostly of 'peculiar motions in the head or between the head and throat' (p. 301). Oddities aside, this account offers an empirical self located firstly in the body and its natural environment, secondly in social relations within a reference group and thirdly in an inner spiritual activity which is really a feeling of bodily activities. These ways of blurring familiar distinctions between me and mine, between self and others and between mind and body are undeniably tempting.

At any rate we now have a broad hint of how to proceed, if we want a social dimension to the self. James himself looked to psychology; but his idea that a man has as many social selves as there are distinct groups about whose opinion he cares is a theme in John Dewey and provides a door into social psychology and so into sociology, unlocked in G. H. Mead's Mind, Self and Society. In general there are, I think, two current lines of sociological thought which might tempt philosophers. One lies in structural role theory, where the self is externalised as the significant typified behaviour of a typified individual and then absorbed into the roles attached to his social positions. When Nicola says to Louka in *Arms and the Man* 'You have the soul of a servant', he gives a minor illustration. The other follows the subjective path from symbolic interactionism, until the self becomes images seen in the eyes of others, reflected to infinity. The pilgrims who tie themselves into R. S. Laing's *Knots* show what can be done. The suggestion is that we cannot understand the self by looking solely to one individual; it exists in relations with others. This idea is not wholly strange to philosophy.

The snag from the philosopher's point of view, however, is that such lines do not yield notions of strict identity. Structural role theory sees the individual as essentially the incumbent of social positions, which, by definition, can have more than one incumbent. There cannot be a position which only I can fill. Even if I am the only person who is the *seventh* king of Ruritania or even if a position, like aerospace adviser to the Ruritanian government, is created specially for me and abolished after me, it remains possible that I might not have held the office without ceasing to be me and that someone else could have held it without becoming me. A list of roles combined in one person can individuate in fact but not principle. (Even if special and magical powers accrue to a seventh king in Ruritania, the logic which stops two people both being the seventh king is not the source of the special powers which make 'seventh king' a position and so secures uniqueness of the wrong kind.) Hence I *am* the sum of my roles only on further assumptions about the relation of identity to roles and these assumptions in turn fall foul of the philosopher's demand for strict identity. Equally a proposal (which would surely delight Leibniz) to define a person in terms of reflections in the eyes of others will merely raise unanswerable doubts about the identity of the others. It may suit R. S. Laing not to know who anyone is but the philosopher protests that such monads cannot be logically unique. Philosophers will deem it neither essential to my being a person that I have social positions nor logically necessary to my being the particular person I am that my social posititons are in sum unique to myself. The sociologist can elaborate until he is blue in the face, adding to my role-set the role-sets of my role-partners and of my role-partners' role-partners, throwing in the historical order in which I played my roles with emphasis on my most formative experiences and even sneaking in mention of genotype and phenotype. These are all factors in my conduct and an intimate part of being me. But the philosopher is implacable. He demands that there *cannot* be two persons who satisfy whatever makes me the particular person I am and the sociologist supplies a notion of who I am too lax to count as identity at all. That seems to be one reason why philosophy and sociology do not commune about identity. Whether or not it amounts to a difference in sense, sociology does not even try to meet the philosopher's criteria and the philosopher deals in nothing which could be *en crise*. Yet the twin puzzle remains that strong actionists need to fill the lacuna in role theory with a self and that philosophers cannot meet their own criteria. Perhaps, then, the philosopher is asking too much or the strong actionist trying too little. Indeed the actionist is certainly trying too little, if the argument of the book has carried any conviction. But, before urging him to greater effort, let us ask whether the philosopher is asking too much. Is he demanding strict, numerical identity, where qualitative identity would serve?

William James would say so and his own solution is therefore instructive. He opens with a section on the feelings of identity which we have for our selves of yesterday and remarks that 'Resemblance among the parts of a continuum of feelings . . . constitutes the real and verifiable "personal identity" which we feel' (*Principles* p. 336). None the less there is a Unity of Consciousness in virtue of which my various selves are mine, just as there is a common ownership in virtue of which cattle are branded with the same mark. The cattle bear the same brand because they belong to the same owner; they do not belong to the same owner because they bear the same brand. So too my various selves need a unity and it consists in 'the real, present onlooking, remembering, "judging thought" ' (p. 338), 'a remembering and appropriating Thought incessantly renewed' (p. 362). 'Personality implies

95

the incessant presence of two elements, an objective person, known by a passing subjective Thought and recognised as continuing in time' (p. 371); 'the identity found by the *I* in its *me* is only a loosely construed thing, an identity "on the whole", just like that which any outside observer might find in the same assemblage of facts' (pp. 372f.). To cut the story short we do find in James the now current idea, that qualitative identity will do. I am the same person I was yesterday in that there is a present Thought which correctly judges that this Me is the same Me; but there is strict identity neither for the Me nor for the I. Identity is always 'on the whole'.

James thus offers to let the strong actionist off the hook. We complained a moment ago of a puzzling lacuna just where there should have been a self to sustain the construction of social reality. Now the complaint seems groundless. There is an old Buddhist image of the self as a series of candles each lit from the stub of the last and, for James, it is enough. To ask more is a mistake, as A. J. Ayer suggests in his elegant refurbishing of James –

If one speaks of the construction of objects out of the flux of experience, it is indeed natural to ask who does the constructing; and then it would appear that whatever self is chosen for this role must stand outside the construction; it would be contradictory to suppose that it constructed itself. But the metaphor of construction is here misleading. What is in question is the derivation of concepts, not the fabrication of the things to which the concepts apply. To 'construct' either the material or the spiritual self is to do no more than pick out the relations within experiences which make it possible for the concept of a self of this kind to be satisfied, and these relations exist whether or not we direct our attention to them.[9]

If James' approach is basically in order, the road is now clear. Basically identity depends on continuity 'on the whole' of both I and Me. Continuity of the I is a matter of feeling, remembering, judging and being aware of inner activity, amounting to a warrant to appropriate past states as belonging

---

[9] *The Origins of Pragmatism*, Macmillan, 1968, part II, chapter 3, p. 261. Among other recent writings in support of a qualitative notion of identity for persons, I am especially struck by Derek Parfit's 'Personal Identity', *Philosophical Review*, vol. LXXX No. 1, 1971.

to my history.[10] Identity of the Me subdivides into identity of the bodily Me, the social Me and the spiritual Me, depending in each case on enough continuity of suitable relations. My body extends to relations with home and family, my social selves are continuously transacted with groups of other individuals, my soul is a set of interrelated experiences; and there is identity to the degree to which I am spared radical simultaneous breaks. This is a psychological account and a highly individualist one. But, if it is basically in order, it could easily be made more sociological. We need only start the Me with the social self, taking groups of significant others as primary (groups 'who recognise him' being then prior to groups 'about whose opinion he cares') and explaining significance in terms of a stock of shared meanings. The spiritual Me becomes the set of social experiences and transactions I am involved in, as filtered through a bodily Me, in turn established by reference to significant others. Finally the I will be the awareness which I bring to transactions, that in virtue of which I can innovate within and upon the shared meanings which secure my identity. Since, like all Pragmatists, James has an active conception of the self, we need only place a sociological level beneath the psychological, to get a robust actionist thesis about the social construction of reality.

But is James basically right to dispense with strict identity and is Ayer right to regard 'construction' as the picking out of relations which exist whether we pick them out or not? Tackled head on, these questions are too hard to settle at a stroke and I shall try an indirect assault presently. But it may be as well to start by seeing why they are hard. James proposes that we think of human identity in a way which fuses what philosophers often take to be distinct questions. For psychologist's reasons he wants it a matter of degree whether different states linked by bodily continuity are states of the same person. It will remain a matter of degree, whatever we do to promote the social Me over the others. For instance James would be willing to describe the onset of schizophrenia as one person becoming two who are the same person as him but not

---

10 Ayer works out a plausible relation of 'appropriating' in *The Origins of Pragmatism*, *loc. cit.*

identical with each other. The apparent contradiction will carry over to a sociological description, like Goffman's, of schizophrenia as a dislocation of the grammatical rules governing social negotiation. Yet there is no self-evident contradiction. It must be shown first that the self-identity of persons is transitive. Test cases from medicine or science fiction seem to beg the question rather than help in solving it.

Direct assault would therefore be a lengthy business. Phenomenology offers no way to by-pass discussion of phenomenalism or Kant's claims for the transcendental unity of apperception. In general it seems disingenuous to suggest that the topic of personal identity will yield much to an enquiry on behalf of our conceptual scheme without going deep into epistemology. We cannot attempt the dive here; but luckily we have a more modest aim. I need to show only that strong actionism must hold out for a strict criterion of identity, when assigning different states to the same person. I shall try to do it by arguing that, without strict identity, there can be no good reasons for action.[11]

The idea before us, I repeat, is that the social world is constructed out of shared meanings by acts of self-definition. Current versions usually make the process a rational one. It is not immediately obvious why. If the idea is that the social world is a myth and that myths are real, then there is point in the romantics' claim that creation is the intrusion of irrational imagination upon rational order. Alternatively, sociologists of knowledge, who find Sorel too flamboyant, commonly make the process non-rational. But strong actionists usually insist that it is rational. When they go on to add that the proposition holds universally, in that social interaction is always among rational agents, there is no escaping an equally universal situational logic to explain institutions and actions. I shall object to situational logic in due course and give warning here only to stop it blocking the path. Alan Ryan has observed, 'The proposition that men act appropriately to their situation or that

---

[11] My original plan was to make the connections from 'outside' by arguing that action cannot be explained in an actionist, programming-model way without strict criteria for the agent's identity. I owe the neater idea of working from 'inside' to Michael Bloch's work on ethics.

they act for good reasons, is such an obvious falsehood that it could only be defended as a conceptual truth.[12] As the target of this pretty shaft, I grant him all but his moral. I shall indeed defend the proposition as a synthetic *a priori* truth but one about autonomous actions. It would be an obvious falsehood that all men always act from good reasons and a plunge into situational logic, in order to save the proposition *a priori*, only makes for vacuity. Autonomous Men, however, do act from good reasons and that, we shall find, is why we need a strict criterion of identity.

To trace this link, I must borrow a point to be defended in the next chapter. It is that *Zweckrationalität* is not a primary or self-contained notion of rationality. The temptation to take it as basic is great. For example, a man buys a train ticket. Has he good reason? That seems to depend solely on whether he has hit on the best means to wherever he wants to go. The rationality of goals seems not to arise, except in so far as one goal is a means to the next. In a sense, indeed, even the objective rationality of means can drop out, if it is enough for the traveller to believe that he has the best route. At any rate, it is usually held that there can be rational action on false belief. Hence *Zweckrationalität* seems a temptingly simple and clear notion, which can be applied without looking beyond internal relations.

Were there no more to be said, no issue of the agent's identity would arise. In truth, however, instrumental accounts of rationality are not silent about the rationality of goals. Trading shamelessly on our every day habit of ascribing rationality to people who act on false beliefs for dotty ends, they pretend silence, where they in fact assume some variant of the Psychological Unity of Mankind. By relying, for instance, on some vacuous universal desire to attain happiness or maximise utility, they can credit the agent with a rational goal, without actually saying so. A presumption is thus created that mere desire for an end counts as a reason for pursuing the end. So let us attack the presumption. Suppose our traveller buys a ticket to Ongar, a horrid place where no sane man would wish

[12] *Proceedings of the Aristotelian Society*, supplementary volume XLVII, 1973, p. 179.

99

to be. His conduct now becomes puzzling, since there is no good reason for finding the most efficient means to achieve something there is no good reason to have done. The puzzle is not really removed by his believing, however falsely, that Ongar is some bosky paradise of yachts and shingled roofs. For, in so far as the false belief is justifiably held, the end has claims to being rational after all; and, in so far as he believes without reason, he has better reason to go somewhere else. Nor can a mere desire to achieve an end he should have known to be dotty constitute a good reason. Nor does it help to remark that there are other reasons for buying the ticket. If he is escaping from an angry tong, then we should have taken more care in specifying the end to which he has the rational means. If the trip is so scenic that the journey is an end in itself, then that might shift the action into the expressive category but then would not show it *zweckrational* after all. Otherwise there remains a hidden presumption that the end will pass muster and, where the presumption fails, the action ceases to be rational.

These stark *dicta* will be supported later, as promised. For the moment, I assume that there is a gap between showing an action to be a rational means and showing it a rational action. In other words it is one thing to prove that $X$ is the best means to $Y$ and another to assert that therefore a man, who does $X$ in order to achieve $Y$, is acting rationally. Equally, even if we allow that a desire for $Y$ is a reason for doing $X$, we are not thereby committed to regarding it as a good reason. The wrong target is better missed.

The gap was clearly seen by traditional political theorists, who filled it with a thesis about our ultimate interests deriving from our essential human nature. Hobbes and Rousseau, for example, did not simply issue prescriptions off the tops of their heads, with wild leaps from 'is' to 'ought'. They held that whatever constitutes us human beings is *pro tanto* something we have good reason to preserve and foster by our actions. Here we might recall the old idea of *conatus*, signifying the endeavour of each thing to persist in its peculiar being and taken by Spinoza as 'nothing else but the actual essence of the thing in question' (*Ethics* III props. VI and VII). In traditional

100

theories a claim about our ultimate interests underpins the analysis of what is, no less than of what ought to be. Such an approach is out of fashion, but, as noted at the start of the book, still lurks in every theory which appeals to the psychological or any other unity of mankind. One does not assert less of a universal claim about human nature by making it specific to economic formations, modes of operant conditioning or given forms of life. Any such ultimate determinants of action still serve both to explain human conduct in terms of the sort of creatures the actors are and to recommend ways of organising life so as to serve human interests. Where the actor is acting in what a theory takes to be his best interests, it will seem as if no question of the rationality of goals arise whereas, in truth, it is presumed to be already settled.

Taking the hint from traditional political theory, we can propose an ambitious thesis about autonomy. An autonomous man acts freely by definition. He acts freely, only if he has good reasons for what he does (and no better reasons for doing something else). He has good reasons, only if he acts in his ultimate interests. His ultimate interests derive from what he essentially is. What he essentially is depends partly on what is essential to his being any person and partly on what is essential to his being that particular person. The thesis will be defended in later chapters but its ambitions are vain unless the concept of 'what he essentially is' is, so to speak, load-bearing. I shall try to show next that the load requires strict criteria of identity for persons, criteria which let the self stand outside the construction.

The concept of freedom I shall need is, in Hobbes' words, that of 'the absence of all impediments to action which are not contained in the nature and intrinsical quality of the agent'[13] – a positive notion, which gestures to a nature and intrinsical quality. To see why, let us recall the toughest version of normative structuralism. Here only role-concepts enter essentially into the explanation of social action, the identity of the

---

[13] Hobbes' letter to the Marquis of Newcastle giving 'My Opinion about Liberty and Necessity', Molesworth edition, vol. IV, pp 272–8. This is not the definition Hobbes gives in chapters 14 and 21 of *Leviathan*. I am borrowing a fine phrase for my own purposes, not for his.

agent, being given by his social positions, is not strict and there are no ends for whose sake the roles are played, beyond those of discharging one's duties. When the agent asks, 'Why should I?' he can be given only the answer which an observer would receive to the question 'Why did he?', namely that it is required by the set of roles and positions occupied. What reason has the agent to accept those positions? Either he cannot escape them or they allow him to occupy some further position. But constraints are not in themselves freedoms and there can be no reason for occupying the ultimate positions. So although, by defining the self in terms of social positions, this theory finds the key impediments to action in the nature of the agent, it denies him any intrinsical quality which allows the requirements to be good reasons. He is a free agent neither within his roles nor without.

This will sound implausible. The recruit may have no good reason for being in the army but he has excellent reason to shine his boots before the sergeant-major sees them. The role of judge may contain no reason for being a judge but it gives good reason for a man who is a judge to wear a wig and live scrupulously. That is true enough but it shows only a weakness in a tough normative structuralism. The recruit's excellent reasons derive only incidentally from the fact that dirty boots signal duty unperformed. To make the fact integral, he needs good reason for becoming a fully-fledged soldier; otherwise fear of the sergeant-major operates viscerally and so outside the structure of norms. Equally, in saying that the judge has a good reason to wear a wig, we presume he has a good reason for being a judge. If normative structuralism cannot produce one, then that shows its limitations.

But we fare no better with the other trend in social thought noted earlier. The characters in Goffman's world are played by actors who treat their roles as public means to private ends. The role yields a stock of reasons for action, which become good reasons in so far as the actor has good reasons for playing the character. So far so good – we are again back in Quentin Skinner's realm of social meaning, with the previous advantages. But we are also in the realm of pure individualism, where individuals enter social relations so well endowed with the essential attributes of human beings that roles are merely accidents. We grant that social relations secure the qualitative identity of characters but, having objected that the self has to be more than a 'repertoire' or a 'code', we still need strict identity for the actors. Goffman's actor is not in the altruistic business of investing effort and ingenuity for the benefit of later 'selves' just like him. He is working for himself, to preserve and foster what is strictly himself from one time and one role to another.

Pure individualism, taking men as the pre-social atoms of classical utilitarian and liberal theory, does offer to make action rational by referring it to goals which are in turn rational because of what the agent is. Its classic snag, however, is that it cannot say what the actor is. It is no answer to Ayer to leave a mere Thing from Inner Space standing outside the construction. Yet an active conception of man must have a final category of creative *self*-expression, not just in ethics but also in the epistemology of explanation. An active construction of the social world by rational initiative needs a purpose derived from a continuing, unmysterious self. Where relations within experience are the work of rational initiative, it is not enough to hold that they 'exist whether or not we direct our attention to them'. Where Plastic Man is content with degrees of identity and individuality, Autonomous Man still needs a strict principle of personal unity.

What is it, then, which can continue numerically the same from one role and social scene to another? We do have a clue. We acquired it on finding that historical explanation is possible only if the reasons for action which the agent has, because he was set a problem as the occupant of a set of social positions, are also his own reasons. For a passive *homo sociologicus* there was no problem, since he was conceived from the start as essentially a creature of his social positions; and distance from one role was always subjection to another. But Autonomous Man was introduced as an actor initially distinct in principle from the characters he plays. The effect, we saw, was to leave it chronically open whether the cap supplied by the historian was the cap actually worn by the actor. There would have been no harm, if there were only a demonic doubt raised. But it also

103

became impossible ever to enter the actor's world at all. Consequently we have only one move. It must sometimes be true that what the character has good reason to do, the actor *eo ipso* also has good reason to do. Necessarily the autonomous actor must be himself in some of his characters.

To avoid slipping back into a passive mode, we must let the autonomous actor choose his self-defining characters rationally. If he is to be, say, an autonomous King of Ruritania, then he must have chosen to make that his essential role and have done so for good reasons. The snag is not that the crown is inherited rather than acquired. For, although he did not choose to be king, he can still choose whether to play with distance. In more fluid societies, there is also a choice of roles and I daresay it is a task for political theory to design a set of roles which would allow every man to be himself. The snag goes deeper. It seems at first that it does not matter what positions the actor is dealt provided that he has a rational way of deciding which positions to identify with, perhaps after moving to other positions which suit him better, Hence it seems that, although he has no real interests in a notional capacity of pre-social atom, he can acquire real interests by identifying with rationally accepted positions. Thus, if it is in the real interest of the king to deal justly with defeated enemies, then it is also in the real interest of anyone who is essentially the king. But, alas, in that case, he must have had a real interest in accepting the role. He cannot acquire his interest along with the role if he is to accept the role rationally.[14]

The snag is a powerful one, affecting, for instance, any theory of justice which tried to make individuals rationally agree to a social contract before they were allotted positions and roles within the contract. Either the individuals had real interests all along or they acquired them with their positions. The former option takes us back to pre-social atoms with, presumably, identical interests or presupposes a hidden prior contract to play the game which results in the visible contract. The latter option makes us wonder how it could have been rational to agree to the visible contract. Since we want to allow

[14] I owe this awkward point to Michael Bloch.

different men different but equally rational paths to self-realisation, neither option is enticing. My own view is that, despite the snag, real interests are acquired within a social contract. The initial choice of position, non-rational in prospect, can be rational in retrospect or, if irrational in retrospect, can be rationally corrected. A man can, I think, have good reason to be glad today that he got married yesterday without thereby having to have had good reason yesterday to be glad at his impending change of state.

At any rate, we can at least secure strict identity by making autonomous men define themselves as characters. Physical actions individuate the agent by netting him into the space–time grid. As noted, this gives us only a strict identity of bodies. But when the individuating actions are essentially those of a character the agent has rationally become, we get a strict identity of particular persons. There are many kings of Ruritania but each does and is responsible for doing a unique set of kingly actions. When the actions are essentially kingly and autonomously those of a particular king, we have the missing relation. He is not just playing king nor is he passively following a script. His different actions are rationally his and also those of numerically the same king. On these terms he achieves a strict identity. No doubt it is always precarious but, while it lasts, it belongs to an active social self standing outside the construction.

In summary, then, there is a 'What's What?' game of identifying physical bodies and, ignoring old puzzles about amoebae and the serial repair of hammers, we presume it can yield strict criteria for physical identity. But it does not contain enough for a 'What's Who?' game of reidentifying persons. Even if having the same body or being the same animal are necessary conditions, they are not sufficient. Prompted by the thought that bodies are just bodies unless relations between them are endowed with shared meanings, we pass to a 'Who's What?' game. Here the shared meanings are externalised and given system in positions and roles. But occupancy of the same positions at different times is neither necessary nor sufficient for being the same person. Yet the 'Who's Who?' game, played with extra-social individual egos, yields only the qualitative criteria of memory. We need a more substantial 'I', one with both personal and social identity. The problem is to make personal identity personal and social identity identity. Our final conjecture is that the strict identity is that of bodies, which in turn secures that of persons who perform individuating actions; their identity as persons is secured by their having rationally become occupants of social positions; where there are no suitable positions, their identity ceases to be strict and they become passive.

If that sounds cumbrous, it does at least explain what a crisis of identity is a crisis of. The affliction strikes when what I am no longer accounts for who I am, because what I do is no longer the rational acting out of what I have chosen to become. The reasons for action supplied to me no longer function as my own good reasons. The threat to my identity is then both subjectively painful and objectively real. Perhaps it can sometimes be removed with inkblots or, for that matter, cold baths, fretwork or community service. But we are not dealing just with a disorder of persons. Autonomy requires a choice of roles in which a man can rationally do his duty. If few men take this course, it is in part because few societies offer it. To create a Good Society where men can be themselves remains a task not for tinkers but for tailors.

# 6

## Elements of action

### PURPOSES, INTENTIONS AND RULES

We have the stage and the actor but not the missing alternative to causal explanation. My favoured candidate is the notion of rationality and I shall maintain that the rational man is both a free agent and a proper subject for science. But other claimants will be considered and will contribute to the conclusion. Human action is purposive, intentional and subject to rules. Each of these ideas has been offered as the key to the social sciences and I shall borrow an element from each. Purposive action is explained by reference to its goal, which need not be reached but affects the way in which the agent adjusts to experience. His intentions are bound up with criteria of sameness and difference for possible actions and are crucial for deciding what he chooses to do and what he prefers it to. The rules he follows belong to an external fabric of roles and interpretations, which partly determine the significance of his actions. Not seeing the key in the notions of purpose, intention and rule, however, I shall treat them eclectically, for the sake of a fuller account of rational explanation. This is no mark of disregard for scholars who have taken a stand where I merely pass through and readers who are unconvinced by the line proposed here will have their own ways of reaching an active conception of man.

To set the task, let us recall briefly why we rejected causal explanations of autonomous actions. Although the correct analysis of Cause is fiercely disputed, we insisted on lines involving the idea of law. If lighting the touchpaper is to cause the rocket to fire, then there is at least a law-like connection

107

between events (or facts) of the two sorts. Whether the connection has to do with necessity *a priori* or *de re* or with no necessity at all, at least it holds universally in the same conditions and explanation consists, to that extent, in assigning the particulars to their general class. Hence derives authority to infer subjunctive conditionals. Autonomous actions, while doubtless having partial determinants of this causal sort, are not done *because* they instance a causal law. Our other cavil was the transitive nature of causal connections. If $a$ is the cause of $b$, which is the cause of $c$, which is the cause of $d$, then $a$ is the cause of $d$. So the cause of the cause of my action would be the cause of my action and the effect of its effect would be its effect. The former clause leaves me too little autonomy and the latter too much responsibility. I do not do autonomously what the past causes me to do; nor am I responsible for what others do autonomously because of what I set in motion. Without repeating the earlier reasoning, I assume therefore that we want a mode of explanation to explain the particular by the particular and one which makes autonomy make sense. An autonomous action has partial causes, no doubt, but it also has more of an explanation than its partial causes can provide.

Our task thus concerns a special group of phenomena and there is a demarcation problem. The first suggestion is that the realm is one where teleology reigns, a realm ordered by purpose and function. Some plants achieve photosynthesis as if solving a minimax-problem for positioning their leaves with the aid of golden numbers; some shoppers maximise their consumer surplus as if *au fait* with the last word in microeconomics. The uniquely long, hard beaks of some Trobriand Island birds are needed for the birds' survival; crime occurs in all human societies and helps to preserve the norms whose enforcement it provokes. Aunt Jobiska's cat stalks mice like an intelligent homing missile; chess masters sacrifice pieces with an eye to the end game. Such examples invite us to find, or at least to postulate, goals at work. The idea is a very broad one. The plant's equilibrium is very unlike the chess master's intention, the consumer's indifference map very unlike the birds' functional needs But perhaps there is advantage in a concept which applies to things and to organisms, to institutions and to men, to the conscious, the unconscious, the merely organic and even the inert. No doubt the category of purposive behaviour would have to be broken down into species or analysed into a battery of typified models. But that is not our business here. Our sole question is about the category as a whole (supposing there is a single category here) and asks whether explanation by purpose does or can conflict with causal explanation.

There is an initial case for distinguishing the purpose of behaviour from its cause. To put it too simply, goals pull from in front and causes push from behind. As Aunt Jobiska's cat prepares to pounce, its hunger is an unrelieved tension, the sight of the mouse a past and present stimulus and the goal, the relief of the tension, a state in the future. We have a system in search of equilibrium. The equilibrium may be dynamic or shifting and may never be reached. But it acts as an antecedent which exists only afterwards and is needed to complete the explanation.

This is careless talk, betrayed by admitting that the goal-state may never occur. If lightning strikes, the cat may never catch the mouse but the explanation of its previous behaviour remains the same. So, it seems, the determinants of behaviour must be complete, without reference to what may not happen. The needs of organisms, the functions of systems, the desires and intentions of agents all operate *a tergo*. Whether or not final causes are final, they are always causes.

The retort is also too simple, however. It is mere sleight of hand to pass goals off as drives or needs. The need of an organism to relieve tension or of a social system to achieve integration is no less an artifice than the magnetic pull of a future state. Such needs can be identified only in terms of how they would be satisfied, thus reinstating the goal as ground of identity for the behaviour. There are, for instance, many ways of hunting food and they share only a common purpose; conversely behaviour without that purpose is not to be identified as hunting food, whatever its other similarities to hunting. If this is too dogmatic, then it can be said at least that there is a great deal more work to be done on the physiology and psychology of unrelieved tensions before they can be identified without reference to goals. Nor is it obvious that such work would have any purchase on human hunting, which belongs in a social, partly ritual, context or on the alleged functional needs of social systems. There may be vacuous 'goals' – a societal goal of integration, for example, derived from defining society in part as a system of inter-dependent processes – but there are also vacuous 'needs'. A similar risk is run by anyone who tries to translate the standing motives of men into dispositions or tendencies. Greed, for instance, can be treated as a disposition rather than a beady eye to a satisfaction in the near future, but it takes effort to ensure that mention of goals does not recur in specifying the disposition.

The last paragraph scored no strategic point but was meant only as a simple riposte to the simple retort. It could perhaps be developed to show that there are final as well as efficient causes but it is no help in arguing that goals are not causes at all. So let us be more precise about the form of teleological explanations. The neatest analysis[1] starts with the thought that purposive behaviour would not occur, were it not necessary to bring about its result. The boiler would not switch on, if the room could reach the set temperature without it. There is a cause for its switching on in the previous state of the thermostat, produced by the low temperature of the room. But there is also a purpose, which lies in the connection between the switching on and its effect. Can we not have a series $S_1$, $S_2$, $S_3$, where $S_2$, can be explained causally by citing $S_1$, and teleologically by citing $S_3$?

If so, that is a very misleading way of putting it. It suggests that the connection between $S_2$ and $S_3$ is not causal, whereas, at least for the central heating system, it is. It suggests also that the actual occurrence of $S_3$ is the explanatory factor, whereas we have already seen that the goal-state does not have to occur at all. The latter point is easily remedied, however, if we say that what explains $S_2$ teleologically is not the fact that $S_3$ will

---

[1] I am here following Charles Taylor's distinguished lead given in *The Explanation of Behaviour*, London, 1964, and 'The Explanation of Purposive Behaviour' in R. Borger and F. Cioffi, eds., *Explanation in the Behavioural Sciences*, Cambridge, 1970. But also see D. H. Mellor's notes on Taylor in *Mind* 77 (1968), pp. 124–6, and *Mind* 82 (1973), pp. 106f.

occur but *the fact that $S_2$ is required for $S_3$ to occur*. $S_2$ is required for $S_3$ in the sense that, if $S_3$ does occur, it will be (in part) because $S_2$ has occurred. While it is a feature of all causal sequences that each member occurs in part because its predecessor has occurred, it is not a feature which normally allows explanation of the earlier by citing the later. The idea, then, is to make it a defining feature of a system that the fact that an earlier state is necessary for a later can be an explanation of the earlier. This absolves the later state from having to occur, since the fact stands, whether $S_3$ occurs or not, and introduces a distinctive style of explanation.

The distinctiveness can best be shown by contrasting functioning with malfunctioning. States which help the system achieve its purpose can be explained by citing the purpose and specifying the contribution. The central heating, for instance, would not keep the temperature in balance without the aid of the states of the thermostat. States which thwart the purpose, on the other hand, must be referred to external factors, for instance to a blown fuse, which stops the boiler responding to the thermostat. Formally, with a system designed to generate $S_1$, $S_2$, $S_3$ and functioning, there is a teleological explanation for $S_2$; but when the system breaks down, there can only be causal explanation of the failure of $S_2$ to occur. Have we here a general basis for distinguishing purposes from causes?

The short answer is No. There is a fatal ambiguity about the idea of an external factor. Lightning striking the thermostat is an external factor, but in two senses. Physically it comes from a distance; logically, it has no place in the design. It therefore presents no problem, But many states of systems are internal in one sense and external in the other. Moreover a design can have effects which it was not meant to bring about. Suppose, for example, the system is inadvertently designed so as to overload a wire, which burns out, causing a fire. Here we have a series of states of the system $S_1$, $S_2$, $S_3$, where $S_1$ causes $S_2$ and $S_2$ is required for $S_3$. The only ground for denying that the fact that $S_2$ is required for $S_3$ is the teleological explanation for $S_2$ is the further fact that the system was not meant to produce $S_3$. Yet it was so designed that it produced $S_3$. The distinction depends on our knowing the purpose of the system – un-

111

mysterious for central heating only because the design has a designer. Consequently there is no *general* distinction to be had between purposes and causes, while we wish to attribute purposes to organisms, processes and systems which lack an author.

Moreover nothing has been said to show that purposes are not causes, as opposed to being causes of a particular kind. Every connection in the heating system is causal and the same is true of the process by which leaves are spaced in a plant or Trobriand Island birds develop long, hard beaks. Teleological explanation in general is a licence to read off causal connections in a special way, and the licence is valid only where there are causal connections to read. This is, of course, no comment on the merits of homeostatic theories in biology, organic notions in social science or other brands of functionalism. Indeed it may help to scotch the old objection that functionalism presupposes mythical needs, drives and goals, by treating purpose simply as a licence to cite causal connections as an explanation of the cause. Admittedly it is a hard further question to say what authorises the licences and how we can judge their claims to validity but that is another story. My point is solely that there is nothing here to stand as a rival to causal explanation.

In summary, then, there are two points to note about functionalist explanations of social processes (and neither is a criticism). Firstly, what counts as internal to the system depends on conceptual assumptions about its purpose. A consensus model, for example, gives an external explanation of conflict by citing factors which a conflict model takes to be internal. Secondly, all processes referred to in both internal and external explanations are, so far, causal. Indeed all causal processes can be given a teleological explanation by invoking a suitable concept to make sense of reading the connection as an explanation of the cause rather than of the effect. There is nothing here to detain us in our search for non-causal explanation. We can ask of any process 'for what purposes?' and get a causal answer.

Matters become more promising, however, when we ask 'for whose purposes?' The pattern of leaves on the tree would be of new significance if it was the work of a tree spirit. Tree spirits are interesting here not because they are hidden ghosts in physical machines but because they are active beings. Hidden ghosts would commit us at once to a dualism of substances and a string of famous headaches. Active beings, on the other hand, commit us, immediately at least, only to a dualism of interpretations. In other words and in keeping with the theme of this book, we can start by regarding our data as neutral, unidentified processes, open in principle to passive or to active interpretation. But to interpret is not yet to explain and, while a passive interpretation can only lead to a passive explanation, the counterpoint does not hold. To interpret within the category of action is not thereby to decide for strong actionism against weak. That depends on whether we treat actions causally and so passively or non-causally (when we have learnt how) and so actively. Teleological explanation can be used in either way and that is why we have found no conflict between purposes and causes. But, by the same token, purposes will not be causes when they are the purposes of active beings. It is this thought which I shall use the concept of intention to explore.

Although we found no snag in using the fact that $S_2$ was required for $S_3$ to explain $S_2$, we also found no clear reason, except where the process had an author. That is the difference here between a wire which melts and causes a fire and a fuse which melts as a safety device. Whether the pattern of leaves is well described in minimax terms is no longer a moot point, if a tree spirit with mathematical talent is at work. It is not the fact that lighting the blue paper is required to fire the rocket which explains my lighting it, but the fact that I know this is required and want to fire the rocket. It is sometimes held that a man's actions can be adequately explained by citing his intentions. This is an overstated claim, I shall argue, but it does point to something crucial for a strong action perspective.

The presence of intention is used in common speech to distinguish action from mere change of state or, indeed, inaction from mere inactivity. The latter case is perhaps clearer. There is always much I am not doing but less I am refraining from doing. I often do not kick Aunt Jobiska's cat but rarely refrain from kicking it. There are many items in the shop which I do not remember to buy but less which I forget to buy. Refraining from kicking the cat is, roughly, intentionally not kicking it, despite a desire; forgetting to kick it is, roughly, having intended to but not taking the chance because no longer aware of having intended. Conscious, definite intentions may not be the only kind but, when present, they appear both to identify and to explain the action done.

That they do indeed identify action seems to me true and important. The same action can often take different forms and the same form express different intentions. There are many ways to insult a bishop and many actions which a bishop would misconstrue if he took them for insults. A man can pray without kneeling and kneel without praying. A bridge sharp can signal a void disjunctively, for instance by moving a finger or scratching an ear, whereas an innocent by-stander can wag or scratch but signal nothing. A man whittling a stick might be trimming a spear, training his wrist or doing nothing in particular. Inactivity too may be inaction and inaction may be intervention. Silence can be eloquent, sins of omission deliberate. Only some of these examples depend on convention but all turn on intention. How the phenomena of human life should be grouped, what counts as doing the same or doing different, depends on the intentions of the actor.

The last paragraph makes its point only loosely. The same action can take different forms, only if there is a way of identifying form independently of intention; the same form can express different intentions, only if intentions can be identified independently of form. Thereby hangs a tangled tale.[2] Initially, perhaps, we tend to regard intention as a state of mind (or brain), its expression as a physical state (or change), and action as the latter described as an expression of the former. But no part of this account bears much examination. If my intention is to insult a bishop, any bishop, not my fat old friend George in particular, who happens to be the Bishop of Sodor and Man and happens to be the bishop I am about to insult, then there are at least half a dozen related but distinct mind (or

---

[2] Two recent books of merited influence are D. Lewis, *Convention: a Philosophical Study*, Harvard University Press, 1969 and A. Goldman, *A Theory of Human Action*, Prentice-Hall, 1970.

brain) states, only one of which is the referent of my intention. Presumably I do not intend to insult a fat man, an old friend, George or the Bishop of Sodor and Man. For even though I shall do each of these things deliberately, they are not essential to identifying my action and do not come into the explanation. I shall not have insulted him *because* he was fat, George or incumbent of that particular see. On the other hand the insulting act has contributing parts. I stride rudely towards him, speak the words with a sneer and curl the upper lip. These are not referents of the intention, although I do them all deliberately and some intentionally. Yet I perform them because I intend an insult and they are essential in context. The tale is too tangled to draw a firm moral from but even cursory reflection suggests a case for holding that the citing of intentions can explain without satisfying the criteria for causal explanation.

The case starts by noting that what a man does may depend on what he intends to do and so accordingly does the classification of what has to be explained. A soldier who dies from straying into a minefield is not a datum for a theory of suicide, unlike a man who swallows a harmless aspirin he genuinely believes to contain cyanide. The difference resides in the intention. Yet there seems no way of identifying a state of intending to kill oneself, beyond calling it a we-know-not-what in virtue of which some action (or inaction) can be truly classified as suicidal. Identifying an intention seems nothing other than correctly describing an intentional action. The case then develops three prongs. A causal law is a contingent connection between distinct contingent events (or facts). But here firstly the *explanans* (the intention) is not a distinct antecedent; secondly it is not contingently connected to the *explanandum* (the action); thirdly, since the agent knows what he is doing without having to know that he is an instance of a class, the connection is not general.

Once again it is a case not quickly settled. Even if intentions are not events or states, they are presumably facts and there is no obvious reason why causal laws should not range over facts. If they are facts, then presumably they are antecedent facts. They are also presumably contingent and, since I may always die with intentions unfulfilled, contingently connected

115

to their outcome. Intentions unfulfilled are not just any old acts unperformed but those acts which I had intended to perform. Even if the agent does have privileged access, we cannot infer that he need know no general laws. He has to know himself before he can be sure that he really does intend what he thinks. Besides, consciousness is not so transparent that he can just intuit what he thinks he intends. He surely has to earn his privilege, by learning about himself, perhaps only after learning about other people. This can all be claimed as causal knowledge. Furthermore, even if there were non-contingent connections between intention and action, that would not threaten a notion of cause which ascribed a non-contingent natural necessity to causal laws. Having myself denied that causal ties are contingent and that facts are independent of theories, I, at least, cannot turn round now and conclude that actions therefore have a non-causal explanation.

The dispute seems to me evenly balanced and, since there is no need to decide it here, we shall leave it balanced. But I do insist on the opening move, that the identity of actions depends on criteria of sameness and difference connected with intentions. The point need not be taken very far. It does not, for example, make intention into an irreducible conceptual primitive. Nor does it land us on a Prospero's isle, where the cloud-capp'd towers, the gorgeous palaces, the solemn temples, the great globe itself are spun from subjective meanings. It is enough to inject a whiff of intensionality or indexicality, whereby actions present themselves for explanation already interpreted according to what the actor meant by them. We said a moment ago that introducing active beings commits us to a dualism of interpretations of data which start as neutral, unidentified, processes. The fact of intention (or intension) does take us beyond unidentified data. But it does not commit us to deciding between active and passive explanations. There are passive accounts of subjective meanings, as we have seen. I insist only that the typical data for explanations are intentional actions.

But identifying intentions is only one step towards explaining action. We can, it seems, know what a man is doing without knowing why he is doing it. Historians can agree on

116

the chronicle of Bolingbroke's assault on Walpole, while utterly divided about how to explain it. Admittedly the border between 'What?' and 'Why?' is often arbitrary, vague or depends on what the enquirer knows already. The mechanic who tells me that I have a loose gimble sprocket tells me why my car will not go, while merely stating for himself a fact to be explained. By noting that Bolingbroke was trying to discredit Walpole, the historian both prepares to explain why, for instance, he spoke so often about patronage and picks out a fact for further explanation. As with acts and their consequences, the dividing marker appears to be planted wherever it suits the context of enquiry. Nor is this improbable, once facts are admitted not to be neutral between theories. Nevertheless I do not accept that only degrees of generality and scope are involved. Even if we can be sure of the actor's intentions only after we have a cogent explanation of the action identified with their help, there is still a difference. The citing of an intention can provide the *explanandum*, I shall contend, but not the *explanans*. 'What?' and 'Why?' are both tests of understanding but social context and theory enter differently.

To introduce the difference, let us consider a remark of Durkheim's from the chapter in the *Rules* called 'The Observation of Social Facts'. Discussing society's need for crime, he writes –

The subject matter of every sociological study should comprise a group of phenomena defined in advance by certain common external characteristics, and all phenomena so defined should be included within this group.

For example we note the existence of certain acts, all presenting the external characteristics that they invoke from society the particular reaction called punishment. We constitute them as a separate group to which we give a common label; we call every punished act a crime, and a crime thus defined becomes the object of a special science, criminology.

This passage shows the virtue and limits of looking to the actor's intentions. The virtue is to make us doubt whether criminal acts can be identified by their external characteristics. Are there not innocents in prison and criminals at large? Those punished comprise neither all nor only those who should have

117

been convicted. The 'should' gestures to the fallibility of police and courts and, more moralistically, to the quirks of a list of crimes which includes soliciting and excludes wife-beating. Equally not all reactions *called* punishment are intended to harm, deter or improve the offender. Imprisoning a vagrant on Christmas Eve is sometimes a genial connivance, whereby an elderly villain will break a shop window and escape a bleak season of good will; but it swells the tally of penal sanctions. Conversely magistrates know very well that being deprived of a licence for a year is more of a punishment for some drivers than for others, although the penalty is *called* the same for all. For such reasons Durkheim can be claimed to rest his theory of crime on the wrong data and the same has often been held against his study of suicide.

But crime and punishment are not to be defined by reference to intention alone. *Mens rea* is not solely an intention to harm; nor is every act which intentionally harms, deters or improves an offender a punishment. Crime is a breach of a rule and punishment the authorised exacting of a prescribed penalty. Burning the statute book might not raise the quality of social life but it would do wonders for the crime figures. Similarly there are no insults where there is no etiquette, no gifts without rules of property, no deviance in the absence of norms. The behavioural allure of an external characteristic perhaps led Durkheim to disregard intention in establishing the sameness and difference of social actions but he was right about the need for external rules and collective representations. I may not be chivalrous if I have a horse but, if Collingwood is to be believed, I cannot be chivalrous without one.[3]

In looking only to the actor's intentions, then, we might be tempted to forget the part played by rules in shaping social action. I am not referring to the pressures of acting within a given set of rules, to the external and constraining character of social facts. Rules do, no doubt, shape action in tangible or psychological ways. But, more to the point, they also govern

---

[3] Or, as Marx observed, 'it is centuries since Don Quixote had to pay for the mistake of believing that knight errantry was equally compatible with all the economic forms of society'. *Das Kapital* vol. I, p. 57 in the Everyman edition – a reference I owe to Tim O'Hagan.

the stock of available actions. When we said before that the criteria of sameness and difference depend on intentions, we were speaking of token actions. Tokens are tokens of a type and sameness and difference for types of action depend on rules. Whether a token V-sign is a rude gesture depends on the actor's intention but the actor needs to borrow from a stock, if he is to succeed in being rude in this way. A stitch in a sampler, a step in a dance, the plighting of a troth or castling on the king's side are intentional actions in accordance with rules. It is rules for sameness and differences of types which permit the Nuer to substitute a cucumber for a sacrificial ox or forbid footballers an offside goal. Nor is it only the enquirer who must know the rules to understand the actor. The actor too knows what he is doing, only because he knows how to go on.[4]

The concept of a rule is intoxicating. It gives us a neat and workable notion of social context. It lets us express systematically those images which are so appealing – that the world is a stage, that roles form a stock, that interaction is a game, that reality is negotiated, that norms create a constraining order. Only because there are rules does the actor have moves to make, cards to play, tokens to exchange. With a concept so powerful we seem hardly to need intentions. What is an intention to $X$ over and above the intentional following of a rule which makes $X$ the next thing to do? Citing the rule both identifies $X$ as a token of its type and explains it. It was the next thing to do; it was done because it was the next thing to do. Is this the end of our search?

Well, there is once again a case for thinking the explanation not causal. As with intentions before, *explanandum* and *explanans* are not distinct contingent facts connected by a natural law. What identifies a flick of the hand as a gesture of greeting or the sign of the cross as a blessing also thereby explains something. The rules of a ceremony include the gestures to be made; to know what the gestures are is to know which ceremony it is. There is a rule because a departure from the usual

---

[4] Peter Winch puts a formidable case in *The Idea of a Social Science*, Routledge and Kegan Paul, 1958. It would be a distraction to discuss it here but my comments will be found in 'Witchcraft and Winchcraft', *Philosophy of Social Science*, 1972.

practice is not so much a rarity as a breach. *Explanans* constitutes *explanandum*; *explanandum* cannot await *explanans*.

Once again, however, there is no quick kill. Defenders of a causal analysis can reply that the same gesture can instance more than one rule and so must be distinct from the particular rule alleged to explain it. They can also retort that causal connections need not be contingent. Another tangled tale results[5] but we can cut across the debate by arguing that the price of letting rules do all the work is too stiff for a strong actionism to pay. There is an initial gap between saying that the rule constitutes the action and adding that it explains the action. To close the gap, we must at least accept sets of rules, under some such title as 'cultures', 'value systems' or 'forms of life', as the data of the last resort. Actors can still change a rule or decide to break one, but only if the changing or breaking of one rule is explained as the following of another. Otherwise the claim of rules to be the final category lapses. Yet even this obeisance to the importance of institutions is not enough. For even granted that the connections thus analysed are not causal, they do not exclude causal connections and do not amount to an explanation without them. For instance, even if there is a proper, non-causal way to conduct a lynching, it is a further step to show that lynchings occur *because* there is an appropriate form of life. There has to be a mechanism as well as a symbolism. The point can be hidden by starting with an assumption that men are constituted by the rules they live under. But the assumption can be dug up and challenged. Unless we challenge it promptly, we lose the space we are saving for an active self.

An instructive moral is that, although an active self needs an alternative to causal explanation, not any alternative will do. Actors who are creatures of rules are still passive, however the tie between rule and action is treated. But the threat just posed is not serious, since there seems no reason to accept that intentions are constituted by rules. To learn which rules Bolingbroke intentionally followed was not to learn his inten-

[5] For a splendidly unrepentant reassertion of Hume see A. J. Ayer, 'Man as a Subject for Science', Comte Memorial Lecture, 1963, reprinted in P. Laslett and G. Runciman, eds., *Philosophy, Politics and Society* vol. III, Blackwell, 1967, which has been of great help in writing this chapter.

tion in following the rules. When a referee disallows an offside goal, there may be nothing more to explain. But when other players send the offender to Coventry, we still want to know why they did what the rules for sending a man to Coventry told them how to do.[6] There is rule-distance, just as there is role-distance, and I see nothing to make us agree that distance from one rule has to be subjection to another. All action is rule-governed but all actors are not. That, at any rate, is what a strongly active conception of man must retort. The thought that men follow rules is itself neutral; but to explain the actor in terms of the rules makes the actor plastic.

Yet we are one step nearer the end of our search. The cap fits but is the actor wearing it? We reject obviously passive answers, like Social Darwinism, structural-functionalism, crude Marxisms and other such brands of *homo sociologicus* or *psychologicus*, even when they make much play with a meaning-system. We also reject, as subtly passive, any theory which makes a system of rules and meanings self-explanatory. But we accept the accompanying gloss. The actor is wearing the cap, if he is indeed following the rules which fit him. That still leaves a practical doubt, to say nothing of a general Other Minds problem, but at least we know what to look for. The actor's context is composed of rules, of which roles are a central example or even, if role theory can fulfil its wildest ambitions, the only example. We accept that the actor acts not only in accordance with the rules but also because of the rules.

None the less the search is not over. For weak actionism, to know that the actor followed the rule because it was the rule is to know why he acted. For strong actionism there is more to it. A weak, passive, reading rests the explanation with the rule. A strong, active, one can only rest with the actor. Why did he put himself under the guidance of that rule? The question seems to call for his motive. But motives, in the sense in which patriotism and ambition are motives, are not sufficient answer. Even patriots need not be blind followers of even the rules which guide the proper conduct of patriots. Adventurers take what lies to hand but it does not explain their choice of means

---

[6] This example was suggested by Nigel Norris.

to say so. In finding a cap which the actor wittingly and willingly wore, we are further forward. But something is still missing.

To understand an action we must both identify and explain it. These steps, however continuous and complementary, are distinct. The notions of purpose, intention and rule have told us much about identity and identification but too little about explanation. Admittedly we might have learnt more, had we been less eclectic, and I repeat that I cast no aspersions on thinkers who see more in them. But I cannot myself distinguish active from passive concepts of explanation with their help alone. An actor can have a purpose and follow rules intentionally without acting autonomously. The rules are his stock; his intention marks his choice from the stock; rules and intentions between them settle the criteria of sameness and difference for types and tokens of action. But if there is no more to discern than a fabric of rules intentionally followed, the threat to the self remains, whether or not the resulting form of explanation is causal. We must therefore deny that explanation has yet been reached. The time has come to play the last card.

## REASONS AND MOTIVES

The Autonomous Man whose conduct is proving so enigmatic is well described in chapter XVIII of *The Prince*:

Everyone admits how praiseworthy it is in a prince to keep faith, and to live with integrity and not with craft. Nevertheless our experience has been that those princes who have done great things have held good faith of little account . . . You must know that there are two ways of contesting, the one by law, the other by force; the first method is proper to men, the second to beasts; but because the first is frequently not sufficient, it is necessary to have recourse to the second . . . A prince, therefore, being compelled knowingly to adopt the beast, ought to choose the fox and the lion; because the lion cannot defend himself against snares and the fox cannot defend himself against wolves. Therefore it is necessary to be a fox to discover the snares and a lion to terrify the wolves. Those who rely simply on the lion do not understand what they are about. Therefore a wise lord cannot, nor ought he, to keep faith when such observance may be turned against him . . . Nor will there ever be wanting to a prince legitimate reasons to excuse this non-observance.[7]

We are looking for an explanatory scheme to cope with a man who is both a lion and a fox.

The actions of this prince have a normative explanation, since

(1) he is a prince whose role requires that he be seen to keep faith

(2) he knows that he is so required

(3) conditions (1) and (2) are his reasons for . . .

well, for what? For breaking faith, when necessary, in such a way as to be seen to keep faith. But there is an ambiguity here. The role requires that he keep faith and, since it includes a duty to retain the respect of his people for their sake, to be seen to keep faith. Yet both barrels could be discharged, only if men were entirely good. 'Since they are bad and will not keep faith with you, you too are not bound to observe it with them.' Hence the prince, who is a fox, is seen to keep a faith which he is actually breaking and so gains the praise he needs in order

---

[7] The Everyman edition, 1908, translated by W. K. Marriott.

to govern under false pretences. The people applaud him for living with integrity and not with craft, while his enemies gnash their teeth at his infidelity.

It looks as if his real reasons for action cannot be those in the role, since he knows that what he does will contradict what he knows he is required to do. But, as I read Machiavelli, it can be the duty of a prince to break faith for the sake of the people. There are apparent duties and real duties, which would coincide, only if men were entirely good. When they are not, the prince must apparently discharge the apparent and really discharge the real. On this reading the subject of the third condition is not an individual playing a prince for his private ends but the prince playing a prince in order to succeed in being a prince. Patriots too can be foxes. Despite the whiff of ethics in talk of real duties, we are still in the realm of normative expectations but with stress on the skill needed to meet them enduringly. Those who rely simply on the lion do not understand what they are about.

The categories of purpose, intention and rule are not enough to cope with a prince who has taken Machiavelli's advice. His purpose and intentions tell us what he is after but, unless so lavishly specified that other concepts are brought in, not why. The rules which he follows in breaking faith can, *qua* social rules, only be those requiring him to keep faith. The hidden rules are rules in the different sense that he has good reasons for what he does next. It is not that he knows how to go on because he is following a hidden rule but rather that he is following a hidden rule in so far as he has strategic reasons for what he does. Accordingly we shall now fasten on the idea of good reasons for action, to see if that will let us grasp what the fox is about.

Despite hints in the last chapter that *Zweckrationalität* is not the primary kind, it remains the clearest starting point. The most rational means to a goal are those which give the actor the highest chance of success at the lowest opportunity cost. Already there are signs of deep water but let us proceed in innocence, assuming the actor to have clear, consistently ordered goals, whose rationality is – for the moment – not in question. Let us assume also that, in calculating the best means to one goal, he avoids or discounts at suitable prices disturbance of the others. In other words let us assume that there is an overall best means. The mere fact that the actor hits on it is not sufficient and perhaps not necessary for his action to be *zweckrational*. What are the missing conditions?

*Sub specie aeternitatis* the only addition is that the actor must know that he has found the best means. He has arrived at it not by guess and by God but by calculation and evidence. This may be a tall order, requiring, for instance, that he solve all the unsettled questions in economic theory; but it is implicit in there being a best means. More interestingly, it is enough. The actor does not need a choice of means, since there may be only one way to proceed, if he is to proceed at all. It does not cease to be *zweckrational* to catch a plane, just because there is no other way to get to his destination. Nor does he need to make a deliberate choice, at any rate on each and every occasion. Like the rational motorist, the rational gymnast, poet, yogi and commissar all need an unthinking control of their vehicles. Otherwise there will always be yet another preliminary decision. It would be foolish so to define the rational man that he cannot get as far as his own front door, condemned to sit barefoot in his bedroom, exhausted by the many decisions involved in shaving and unable to decide which sock to put on first. Habit can be rational.[8] There is no snag, provided the actor is also in the habit of monitoring his habits to check for changes in himself and his surroundings. He must respond with fresh habits to growing deaf or a rise in bus fares. But he need not be constantly checking, lest his habitual actions become non-rational.

Since omniscience is rare, we also need an account *sub specie humanitatis*. We can get one either by a slight relaxing of what has just been said, to allow for our finitude, or by recasting the rational decision in terms of what seemed best to the actor. Since we often speak of rational actions done from false belief after imperfect reasoning, the latter option looks tempting. The conditions are now wide open. It is not just that a man can now rationally catch the wrong bus, although even the right

---

[8] The point is well argued by John Dewey in *Human Nature and Conduct*, New York, 1922.

bus was still objectively a less efficient means than the train. It also now becomes permissible to tamper with the rules of reasoning. Subjectively speaking, a rational man can now reason aright from false premises, reason imperfectly or even reason by other standards from premises whose truth is judged by other criteria. The last possibility leads to a general relativism, which we shall rebut in the next chapter. Suffice it to say here that it would make all action equally rational: necessarily, there would be a description of the situation and its logic from the agent's point of view, under which the action done was best. But we need not go so far to get an analogous result. Without tampering with any standards, we could insist that an agent acts rationally, provided he does what seems to him best in the light of what seems to him true. If he thinks he is a poached egg and wants or thinks he ought to sit on a piece of toast, then he seats himself rationally. The result is again to make all action rational and so to rob us of any hope that a man's real reasons will, under certain conditions, yield the explanation of his actions. By saturating the description, we empty the explanation, in readiness for a causal account of wants and beliefs. Subjective rationality is not strong enough to sustain a notion of autonomy.

Yet it can surely be rational for a man to take an umbrella, even though it is not actually going to rain? Indeed it can. But what makes it rational is not the mere fact that he believes it will. The rational man takes an umbrella not because he believes it is likely to rain but because it is likely to rain. We are inclined to fancy that, since rational action can result from false belief and since false belief does not correspond to a fact, the reason for the action must be the false belief itself; and then we are inclined to argue that the same goes for true belief; hence, we conclude, truth or falsity is beside the point. After all, when our man learns later that it had not been even likely to rain, he does not start to wonder why he took his umbrella. That is true enough. But he remains complacent, because he is confident not that he did expect rain but that he was justified in expecting rain. The effect of appealing to a justified false belief is to make whatever he cites in justification into the reason for his action. The facts from which he inferred that rain was

126

likely move up and do duty for the, alas non-existent, fact that it was likely.

The case is quite different where there are no supporting facts either. No doubt he tries to move up a further set in the same way. Although the sun blazed in a clear sky, he heard what he now knows to be distant lorries and took them for thunder. The weaker his excuse, the less justified his action and the nearer he comes to the poached egg man. Eventually he is reduced to offering in explanation the mere fact that he expected rain. Now there is a new fact to explain in another way. For, while he could cite good reasons for expecting rain, he explained both why he expected it and why he took an umbrella. In citing bad reasons, he explains at most why he took the umbrella. We must not be distracted by our habit of accepting objectively bad reasons as good-from-the-agent's-point-of-view into confusing distance from the ideally rational with distance from the ideally irrational. In so far as he acted rationally, he had reasons of some merit, although of less than the thought, for both belief and action. In so far as he resembles the man in search of buttered toast, his beliefs caused his action and the cause of his belief is as yet unknown.

This distinction between reasons and causes will seem flimsy. Surely good evidence causes belief which causes action? I think not. In 'he knew it was likely to rain because the barometer showed it' and 'he took an umbrella because he knew it was likely to rain' neither 'because' exemplifies the law-like, transitive relation of cause and effect. Knowledge of a fact is not to be analysed as true belief caused by the fact. When my phone rings, I may truly believe it is George, but without reason to expect him or to justify claim to psychic powers, I do not know it is him. Equally I believe truly that there is no highest prime number but what causes this belief, if anything does, is the proof and not the fact. The predicates 'true' and 'justified' do not attach to beliefs as 'painted green' attaches to doors. Admittedly I know a fact, only if there is such a fact. But the fact is not the cause of a state of mind but the reason for judgement. Knowledge is a matter of how belief is justified. In ideal cases, my reasons are facts combined with proof of relevance; in less than ideal cases, the facts are incomplete and the proofs partial; whatever is beyond the scope of the ideal is fair game for a causal account.

There are, no doubt, ways of causing belief and action. By hypnosis an insurance agent can, let us say, be brought to sing Clementine because his boots seem tight. Here the cause of the cause of his action is the cause of his action and the sequence can be repeated in similar conditions. If asked for his reason for singing, he replies that his boots feel tight. Crucially neither the merit of the reason nor the truth of the reply comes into it, while the case is one of hypnotism. The law-like connection explains the sequence and the reasons, however good, are rationalisations. Conversely, however, where good reasons do explain action, they also explain any relevant general connection. For example, if it is rational for a chessplayer to play 30.Q–Kt3 ch for the sake of a smothered mate in five, then all rational players so placed would do the same. But it is not thereby true that 30.Q–Kt3 ch is played *because* all rational players would do the same. On the contrary, all rational players would also play it because it is the best move. It would put the cart before the horse to collect a bag of cases of 30.Q–Kt3 ch and then explain all before explaining any. For, as emerged with intentions and rules, the cases in question would not be, absurdly, all cases of 30.Q–Kt3 ch. They would be moves equivalent in context to 30.Q–Kt3 ch in its context and the equivalence would consist in their leading to a smothered mate. (Nor would there be many, since the smothered mate is so famous a trap that players skilled enough to spring it are skilled enough not to give their opponent the chance.) The rationality of the single case is prior to and sufficient for whatever is to be said about the general.

If good reasons were causes, they would operate through law-like connections. The critic will doubtless complain that they do.[9] From –

(1) A rational agent does A in conditions C
(2) George is placed in conditions C

[9] The objection is put by C. G. Hempel in *Aspects of Scientific Explanation*, the Free Press, 1965, section 10, especially 10.3.1. See also his 'Reasoning and Covering Laws in Historical Explanation' in S. Hook, ed., *Philosophy and History: A Symposium*, New York, 1963, reprinted in P. Gardiner, ed., *The Philosophy of History*, Oxford Readings in Philosophy, 1974.

it does not follow that George will do $A$. For that we need –

(3) George is a rational agent

and now 'rational' is doing no work and can be replaced throughout –

(1) An insurance agent does $A$ in conditions $C$

(2) George is placed in conditions $C$

(3) George is an insurance agent

is just as valid. Hence, it seems, what rational agents do is no less a matter of finding laws than it is for insurance or any other agents. There is, however, a key difference between 'a rational agent plays the move which forces a smothered mate' and 'an insurance agent sings Clementine when his boots are tight'. The inclusion of 'rational' is a compressed gesture to there being good reasons for the move. The best move in chess is necessarily the best move and I shall argue later that it is always *a priori* what is rational in given conditions. What insurance agents do, by contrast, is an empirical question. Supposing, for the sake of argument, that they are wont to sing Clementine when their boots are tight, then either there are no grounds for trusting the mere generalisation, or there is some bizarre causal law with this consequence or there is some unexpected good reason to explain it. If, but only if, there is good reason, the form of connection is –

(1) A rational insurance agent sings Clementine when his boots are tight

(2) George's boots are tight

(3) George is a rational insurance agent.

'Rational' has now reappeared. It still occurs inessentially in the argument but it is essential for using the argument as an explanation.

We are not yet home and dry, since 'Insurance' also occurs essentially in both the rational and the causal explanation. Similarly, 'Protestant' occurs essentially in a causal theory which explains suicide rates as a function of the level of social integration, since it is the point of adhesion in explaining the suicide of a pipe-smoking Protestant barber. So it is not essential occurrence which makes 'rational' a peculiar predicate. Nor is it the fact that true statements of what is rational to do are *a priori*, if we were right to conclude in chapter 3, that causal

connections are also necessary. (Readers who remained convinced that causal laws are contingent are spared this concern.)
But there is a further difference. Causal laws about insurance
agents are of the form 'All $X$ are $Y$' and claims to have found
one are testable (even on our interpretation, likening them to
mathematical conjectures). If, however, we say to a neo-
Classical economist, 'Here are some rational businessmen; let
us test your theory by seeing if they equate marginal cost with
marginal revenue', he can object that they are rational, only if
they supply whatever quantity makes $MC = MR$. Since he can
prove it, we can challenge only his assumption that profit is a
rational goal and this would take us out of the realm of
*Zweckrationalität*. Theories prescribing the rational thing to do
are criticisible but not testable as causal theories are testable.
'Rational' does not attach to businessmen as 'Protestant'
attaches to barbers.

The distinction just drawn is contentious and I undertake to
defend it in the next chapters. Here I wish to note two points,
in anticipation. Firstly, Durkheim's influence is a complicating
factor, since the argument of *Suicide* is not conducted quite by
the *Rules*. Besides involving a notion of cause which conflicts
with much in positivism, it also relies on reconstructing the
world of the ill-integrated from within, so as to make suicide a
(semi-)rational act. Consequently it does at times rely on the
explanatory model which I have just seemed to contrast it
with. Secondly economists do very often take their models to
be descriptions of all or most business behaviour. I am not
trying to say this is a mistake but I do think it can obscure the
role of rationality assumptions in applying and allegedly testing the models. As a result we shall end this chapter with much
unfinished business; but, meanwhile, I hope the reader will
suspend judgement about the scope of the emerging theory of
rational explanation. At present I am trying solely to produce
an ideal type which is not causal, for the sake of the twin thesis
that rational action is its own explanation and that departures
from it have a causal explanation.

So far, then, we find that it makes a difference to the explanation of an action whether it was done for good or for bad
reasons. The nub is insultingly simple. That $A$ was done from

good reasons is, in the ideal case, a fact needing no explanation; that $A$ was done from bad reasons is a different fact, needing an explanation. Someone will no doubt complain that the ideal case is impossibly ideal. It involves two sets of true judgements, one by the actor, who must know exactly what he is about, the other by the enquirer who must see through the actor and then judge his action. The economic historian, for instance, has not only to unearth previous theories of money but also to assess their merits. In the present state of monetary theory, this demand would stop him in his tracks and must surely be outrageous?

In reply, there is no methodological snag about outrageous demands. Where they are not met in full, the scope of a rational explanation is diminished to that degree. The actor is only partly revealed and the enquirer speaks tentatively; but the form remains the same. A historian of Free Trade might begin, 'It is far from certain what would have been a sound trade policy in the 1840s but, judged against Professor Samuelson's recent theories, the Manchester school sets us the following problems of explanation.' This approach seems both arrogant and misdirected, on the grounds that we have no business setting 1970s examinations to 1840s candidates, especially when we cannot answer the 1970s paper ourselves. But there is no escape, once we agree that rationality matters, and that a mere logic-of-the-situation will not do. The historian must lay his bets. He will, naturally, point out how he is laying them and record his confidence in them. But he cannot be wholly charitable. If he lays no bets, he will not know what needs explaining. The argument for saying that he must work as if he had the objective truth (using hypotheticals where hesitancy is called for) is not yet complete but it is not blocked by the finitude of human actors and enquirers.

Action is objectively *zweckrational*, then, if it is the overall best means, and subjectively *zweckrational* in so far as the actor had objectively good reasons for judging, perhaps wrongly or perhaps merely on thin evidence, that he had found the best. I may have seemed to presume that, if George takes an umbrella, knowing it to be the best way to keep dry, then we know why he took one. If so, it is high time we stressed the premise stating that he wants to keep dry. The good reasons must be the actor's own reasons and that raises the question of motive. I left the topic bristling with loose ends in chapter 4 and shall now honour my promise to return to it. A motive, viewed for our purposes as a desire defined in terms of its object, can be treated, I shall maintain, as the actor's real reason, defined in terms of his interests.

Following Quentin Skinner before, we agreed that the explanatory value of Bolingbroke's professed principles did not depend on whether he professed them sincerely as a patriot or cynically as an adventurer. We were then tempted to hold, with Skinner, that, in recognising good reasons for action which apply to him, the actor makes those reasons his own. On reflection, however, this let us fit the head to the cap but not the cap to the head; and it created a dangerous dualism, with only the mysterious actor able to pass through the swing doors leading to his inner sanctum. Similarly the prince, who is a fox, leaves no overt clue to his motives; but, unless we can be sure that he has some motive consistent with his use of legitimate reasons to excuse his non–observances, we have not explained what he is about. Although we must expect to be faced with a problem of Other Minds, we cannot afford to leave the springs of action beyond all possible reach.

In fact Skinner's reckoning was not wholly silent about motive. Bolingbroke might be a patriot or a rogue but not, say, a coward or a misogynist. In other words possible motives are restricted by the explanatory claims of the ideological context and, conversely, the explanatory claims presuppose some suitable motive. Moreover each choice of tactics in the campaign against Walpole needs some motive – a desire to keep allies, for instance, or to divert suspicion – to account for the detailed choice of legitimating reasons within the legitimating reasons for the broad strategy. Skinner seems to know more about Bolingbroke's motives than he is letting on, which is just as well, if history is to be possible.

Bolingbroke, then, is too convenient a case, since it makes no difference why the goal was chosen. Equally it is too conveniently obvious why George does not want to get wet. So let us return to the man who desires to sit on buttered toast.

We have already decided that his action is not made *zweckra-tional* by his mere belief that he is a poached egg. Mere desire is equally not enough. He has no good reason for doing in the best way what he will have no good reason to have done. Indeed where there is good reason not to have done something, there is good reason for not taking the best means to do it. If I have good reason to lose my game of chess against the chief of police, then I have good reason not to play for a smothered mate. If mere desire seems a good reason, it is because we assume that doing what we want is good for us. If sitting on buttered toast is a mistake, then a desire to sit may be a cause but it is not a good reason. *Zweckrationalität* too is not wholly silent about motives and ends.

The point is not contentious, while immediate goals are simply means to a further end. The figure shows a railway

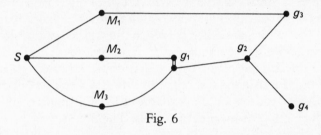

Fig. 6

map, with the traveller at $S$, with a choice of three trains. The best route to $g_1$ is $M_2$, but why does he want to go to $g_1$? If as a step to $g_2$, he will do better to go *via* $M_3$, which offers a through train, despite its longer first stage. The same applies if $g_2$ is a step to $g_4$; but, if $g_3$ is the final destination, then $M_1$ is the best route all along. The calculation need not be solely one of speed or length. Perhaps one route is scenic, another dangerous and the third equipped with the only dining car. Utility theory does not have to deal in crude quantities. Linear programming, critical path analysis and cost–benefit studies apply, at least in principle, to the beautiful life or the cure of souls. Although not all human problems are definable or open to rational solution, *Zweckrationalität* applies to any series of means and intermediate ends.

Where the railway analogy holds, motives can be construed

133

as reasons for pursuing immediate goals. The motive and the reason for an action do not answer the same question in different ways but different questions in the same way. In a Whodunnit, the villain may seem to have both a motive (he wanted her money) and a reason (he already had weed-killer) for poisoning his wife; but the motive explains why murder was better than divorce and the reason why poison was the best method. The motive explains the killing and the reason the poisoning. But characters in thrillers are not the only speakers of English and this way of distinguishing does not always sound natural. Gratitude, for instance, is a common enough motive but would be implausibly presented as a desire to achieve the satisfaction of having paid a debt. The preserving of honour is a motive for fighting a duel by reason of an insult but is not exactly a terminal state. As A. J. P. Kenny observes, a motive is often a 'backward-looking reason'.[10] R. S. Peters remarks very plausibly that motives are in part 'reasons for action which are asked for when there is an issue of justification as well as explanation'.[11] To some extent these are points of language and I do not propose to make natural-sounding English the test of truth. But they also cast doubt on the place of motives in a *zweckrational* scheme, in particular on the distinction of means from ends. The doubt is to be taken seriously.

Granted, then, that we dare not stay silent about motives, there seems every advantage in treating them as reasons of some sort. They fall in neatly under the principle that a rational man, in recognising good reasons for action which apply to him, makes those reasons his own. But there is trouble looming over the rationality of ends and the general means–ends division. The thought that rational means need rational ends is not rendered harmless by treating ends as means to the next end. Indeed this positively invites the obvious question about ultimate ends. There will have to be some, since otherwise a recursive definition of rational action as the rational means to a rational end is viciously regressive. 'Rational means to a rational end' can be taken as 'rational means to a rational means

---

[10] *Action, Emotion and the Will*, Routledge, 1963, chapter 4.
[11] *The Concept of Motivation*, Routledge, 1958, chapter 2.

to . . . to a rational end' but not as 'rational means to a rational means' *tout court*. If the ultimate ends are irrational or non-rational then, by the previous argument, the means cease to be rational. This is not to deny that utilitarian and instrumental accounts of rational action can be used in *causal* explanation, without assigning rational goals. But Autonomous Man is relying on the slogan that rational action is its own explanation and he must be found ultimately rational goals.

What reason could a man have for choosing between goals which are not means to further goals? The easy answer is 'None', since whatever rational result is attained by the choice *eo ipso* makes the goal not a final one, To elude it, we must make some goals desirable for their own sake. But, even granted that it is rational to do what is desirable for its own sake, we cannot avoid giving a fresh sense to 'rational'. That is why I think it a mistake to treat motives solely as reasons for strategic choice, thus ignoring their connection with desires. To bring the mistake out, let us reflect on the problem of the Determined Voter.[12]

This is the puzzling fellow who turns out in winter sleet to vote in an utterly safe seat. He admits cheerfully that his candidate will lose (or win) by twenty thousand votes or so. He agrees that his fireside is snug and television enticing. But he votes just the same. No doubt it is tempting to find him a further end. He might be hoping to save the loser's deposit or to impress his neighbours. Perhaps he has to face other party workers in the bar afterwards. No, he insists with the smug humility of the good citizen, he voted solely on principle. Well, on what principle? He has no legal duty in Britain and we may coherently suppose that his mates see no moral duty either. But it explains nothing to credit him with a private principle that the good citizen always votes. This tells us merely that he votes because he thinks he should and that is precisely what we are trying to explain. Being one of these odd

---

12 I am prompted by Stanley Benn's doughty paper, 'The Problematic Rationality of Political Participation', forthcoming in the proceedings of the 4th Bristol conference, edited by S. Körner, and more generally by Brian Barry's *Sociologists, Economists and Democracy*, London, Macmillan, 1970 and the standard references cited there. See also S. Benn and G. Mortimore, eds., *Rationality and the Social Sciences*, London, Routledge, 1976.

animals myself, I hope the 'because' is a rational one but I can find no instrumental reason. I desire to vote but that mere fact does not make the action rational. Does anything?

The casting of such a vote is an act of expression and falls, by the test of *Zweckrationalität*, into the category of the non-rational. If there is no more to be said, it is then beyond rational explanation and the worthy voter cannot be acting autonomously. Earlier we saved habitual action from this fate by pointing out that habits can be essential skills for pursuing our ends and can be intelligently monitored. But that restored habitual action (sometimes) to the *zweckrational* category, whereas acts of expression are done for their own sake. The area promises to be a large one, if it is right to include all 'traditional' actions in it, all that is done *in more majorum* for the sake of observing a traditional code. Equally ritual actions appear to be essentially acts of symbolism and of witness, done because required by a form of life. Religious conduct too is not easily found a goal to which it is instrumental, granted that pie-in-the-sky explanations are more cynical than just. There are, admittedly, famous attempts to treat expressive acts as instrumental and I am not trying to take sides for or against, for instance, *The Golden Bough*. My question now is whether this is the only way to make the non-rational rational. Can an act of affirmation not be rational in some other sense?

The expressive acts which interest me here are those where the actor affirms his identification with the character. The Determined Voter is declaring his citizenship or, if the party label matters, his loyalty. He is not, I think, acting out the conclusion of a practical syllogism with the major premise that all citizens should vote. His act seems to me one of *self*-expression, signifying not that an individual subscribes to a principle but that he defines himself as a (party) voter. Supposing, at any rate, that there are such acts, can they be rational? The snag is one we have met before and can be put as a dilemma. On the one hand the actor, *qua* atomic, pre-social individual, has no reason to adopt one identity rather than another. On the other hand, in so far as a man follows the rules of a form of life solely because they are the rules he finds himself under, the 'because' is causal and he is passive. So it seems that an act of self-expression is either arbitrary or an abnegation of self.

The only move I can see is, once more, to invoke the idea of real interests which the actor acquires with those characters in which he is himself. We are again back with Bradley, caught, like him, between chapter v of *Ethical Studies*, proclaiming the virtue of accepting my station and its duties, and chapter vi, which confines the virtue to ideally just societies and speaks of a 'non-social ideal', for instance 'the realisation for myself of truth and beauty'. The steps ascending to these uplands are unavoidable. What starts as a search for an active model of man leads first to a demand for actions which are self-explanatory because fully rational, thence to an account of rationality in terms of real interests, thence into ethics and finally to that ancient problem about the nature of the Good Society. Yet it should come as no surprise that questions in ethics and politics attend an analysis of human nature. We cannot know what is rational without deciding what is best.

These connections are plain, where autonomous action is equated with fully rational action. For that plainly prevents our regarding action as rational merely because the agent desires to do it or believes that it is appropriate. As soon as we place the agent in control of what he believes and desires, rational action has to be done from rational belief and rational desire. Hence 'motive' can be construed as 'real reason' but only provided that the real reason moves him to action because what he desires is in his real interests. These are extremely strong conditions, whose effect is to make autonomy a limiting case. I do not think this an objection, unless the limiting case is the only case. There is no harm done, provided actual cases can differ in degree of autonomy. Both actor and enquirer must lay their bets but there is no reason to doubt that some bets are more shrewdly laid than others. It is not absurd to judge some actions more rational than others, while living with the possibility that the judgement may have to be revised. Nor does it make the judgement merely subjective. But the critic, even if he accepts this defence, is likely to remark that all could have been avoided by a less ambitious account of rationality. This I wholly dispute.

The key argument is that rationality is not just a measure of consistency. Rational action can follow on false belief or misplaced desire but only when the belief is rationally held or the desire rationally supported. Objective standards are being invoked, even though we have to bet what they are. So there is no escaping a notion of real interests. Autonomous men are moved not by mere desire but by desire for what is truly self-expressive. The twin effect is to dethrone instrumental and promote expressive rationality. The Determined Voter is essentially a citizen and his action one of self-expression. He has to have an essential social state because a pre-social abstract individual has no reason to adopt one identity rather than another; *self*-expression is needed because his ultimate reasons can only lie in his nature and intrinsical quality. Rational ends have to be those rightly pursued for their own sake and to be expressed in every action which has a rational motive, We can say no less, if the actions of an autonomous man are indeed to be their own explanation.

Very well, the critic replies, the thesis is special to this limiting case; mere mortals act rationally under far weaker conditions. We invited the retort, when we defined freedom for Plastic Man as the absence of frustration, thus apparently doing away with a need to consider the rationality of his ends. If mere mortals have none of these grandiose real interests, we are excused solving every problem in ethics and politics before deciding whether it is rational to use an umbrella in the rain. Or so it seems, until we examine the claim that freedom for Plastic Man is the absence of frustration. As presented in chapter 2, it was implied by passive conceptions of men. Granted that human action is a natural and determined phenomenon, the distinction between free and unfree action is that the former secures whatever the actor happens to want, without frustrating whatever he wants more. This is a point about explaining action in the passive mode. But it is none the less also a thesis in ethics and politics. What is sauce for the assertion that my interest lies in 'the realisation for myself of truth and beauty' is also sauce for its denial. To deny that affluent workers have an ultimate reason to take their place in the class struggle can only be to assert that they have an

138

ultimate reason not to. The point gets hidden partly because ultimate reasons are hard to come by and partly because health, wealth and happiness are such popular goals. But to assume is not to eliminate. Passive conceptions too tell us what we must do to be saved. If they are wrong about freedom, then they are also wrong in equating rational means with rational action.

I do not want to end the chapter in the mists of ethics. Our model of autonomy is meant as an explanatory model. The test case is the prince who is both a lion and a fox. We picture him as a character and as an actor. In the character of the prince, he has a role and duties, in particular those of exercising princely power, keeping faith and retaining respect. He can discharge his duties only if there is a normative explanation of his actions. I do not mean that citing the duties is a complete explanation, still less a causal explanation. That would lead straight back to a passive version of normative structuralism. I mean that his duties are reasons for his action, this fact making them his reasons, once we have the rest of the picture. In a corrupt world he must deal with knaves and so cannot discharge all his duties, as stated. In particular, if he keeps faith and acts liberally, he cannot exercise power and retain respect. He escapes the impasse by seeming to keep faith, where he can keep up appearances and by finding legitimate reasons to break it, where he cannot. Consequently the reasons supplied by his role are to be seen as legitimating devices and, although they are none the less genuinely explanatory, they are not in themselves his reasons. We do not yet know why he interpreted the role as he did. We need his motives or real reasons. Now there is a danger. If we regard him as a pure individual, a hidden, abstract ego, his motives become not only wholly inaccessible but also ineffable. We must be able to know the sorts of things he knows about himself. Since we know only how he appears on some stage, even a private stage must still be a stage. He must be always in some character. Hence we are looking for his real reasons *qua* prince, not his hidden urges but his calculations of real interests. In so far as he has calculated well and found the interpretation of the role which best serves his real interests, we have a complete explanation. In so far as we judge him unjustified, we want a causal explanation of the residue. False consciousness has causes; true consciousness is its own explanation.

We now have an ideal type of enquiry. The enquirer starts by supposing the actor autonomous and by looking at the social stage and ideological context. He identifies the actions as tokens of rule-governed types which apply to positions and roles. He shows why they were required or at least legitimate. So far, posing as a normative structuralist, he has discovered what was done and what still needs explaining. Then he looks for the actor's own reasons. Posing as a methodological individualist, he asks why it suited the actor to do his duty or to present his duty as he did. If all goes well, the action emerges as *zweckrational*, subject to assumptions about goals. The actual goal need not be determined, provided the alternatives all require the same means on the public stage. But the actor still needs to be found good reasons for his choice of goals. The enquirer looks for further goals to which the immediate goals are means. But he has to judge ultimate goals. At this point he recalls that individualism is unintelligible. His final move is to restore the actor to the stage by treating his action as rational self-expression on the part of an essentially social man. The ultimate goals are those of the prince. By now he has probably reached his limit. There is no fully rational course of action or the actor has not found it or the enquirer is so unwilling to bet that he is ready to try a causal mode of explanation. But, at whatever point he changes from active mode to passive, he cannot avoid determining what still needs explaining. The residue is always a departure from an ideal type.

This galloping intellectualism will be reinforced later. But it does not amount to monomania. I am not saying that all actors always act autonomously. Nor, therefore, am I saying that all rules and institutions result from deliberate contracts. My claim is, more modestly, that the intellectualist must be allowed to try his hand first and that he sets the problems. But I do believe that he can also solve some of them. Human beings are puzzle-solving animals and I see no reason to regard most of their solutions with contempt. The prince is a neat case but not one implying that commoners are fools. Nor do I suppose that the mass of mankind are so helplessly trapped in ruling ideologies and false consciousness that only a structural determinism can explain their antics. With institutions as they are, the best solutions that men can find to their everyday puzzles may be imperfect. But lack of power is not to be thought of as stupidity.

At any rate we now have our two models of man and can turn to their bearing on epistemology.

# 7

# The rational and the real

However the honours are finally shared between active and passive, we have asserted the existence of a domain of rules, intentions and reasons and of actors who try to do the rational thing. But we must not assert in ontology what, as epistemologists, we could not possibly know to be true. It is time to pay our epistemological debts by honouring those promissory notes on the bank of Reason.

The debts will be paid with a defence of rationalism. So let it be clear that rationalism has three distinct senses. The blandest is marked by a broad belief that there is the sort of order in experience which makes science possible. J. S. Mill was once described as 'the high priest of rationalism' in this sense, without impugning his robust empiricism. It would be a motley alliance got by lumping together all who thought science possible and their disagreements about the kind of order required would be more instructive than their agreement on the fact of order. Only sceptics, romantics, mystics and a few other champions of the random, the fragmentary, the spontaneous and the ineffable would be debarred. But I mention this sense of rationalism not from mere nostalgia for the rationalist societies who used to sneer at the Trinity in damp, gaslit halls. There is also a present danger in radical critiques of orthodox social science, in the heady relativism brought on by intoxication with paradigms and in recent fulminations against method. It is the danger of so undermining claims to objective scientific knowledge that not even rational preference for one conclusion against another is left. I shall try briefly to stave it off later in the chapter.

Secondly 'rationalist' is sometimes used to label theories of

143

action which rest on assuming rationality in men. There are many ways to construe the assumption and this book endorses one of them. Such theories place some sort of divide between natural and social sciences and we shall ask where and how deep it should go. They also prompt the thought that the social sciences are somehow normative. But it is one thing to say that norms are an ineliminable part of the subject matter, another to deny that the social scientist can have a value-free standpoint and yet another to detect normative implications in the findings of social science. These topics too will get a share of attention.

Thirdly, my central claim is for rationalism against empiricism. There is an old epistemological dispute about the scope of reason and experience in justifying claims to knowledge of the world. Hints were dropped in chapter 3, which set off from a crudely empiricist idea that truth always lies with contingent facts, independent of all theory, and ended with a loose plea for the bearing of 'conceptual necessities' on experience. The old dispute remains, to my mind, as crucial as ever. I do not think it undercut by pragmatism, which I regard as a fresh empiricism, nor by conceptual analysis, which, I would maintain, does take sides after all, nor by post-Kuhnian philosophy of science, which I find naughtily ambivalent. But I say this by way of nailing my colours to the mast and I recognise that such developments have made the old epistemological dispute too subtle and elusive for quick answers. There is, alas, no space for proper treatment and the reader is welcome to conclude with a shrug that we are all rationalists nowadays. But I shall try to show that the scientist must make assumptions which experience cannot fail to confirm and shall argue that only rationalism can make an honest woman of them.

These three senses are not to be confused. That all science needs a rationally ordered subject matter, that social science is essentially concerned with rational action and belief, that knowledge of principles of rational order is *a priori*, are wholly distinct assertions. None the less I shall risk confusion by starting with a topic which bears on all three. It is the topic of Other Minds, treated here as the question of how we can know that we have rightly understood the meaning of another's action.

The plan is to extract some general assumptions from the special case of understanding another language and to show that they apply throughout the understanding of action and belief. Then, in the next chapter, it will be asked what sort of understanding is involved and what is to be demanded of a theory of knowledge which justifies such assumptions. There will be an oblique, epistemological discussion of *Verstehen* and ideal types, with the former seen not as empathy but as the kind of *a priori* knowledge needed to grasp the latter. Then, in the final short chapter, the thesis of the book will be rehearsed and its limits admitted.

Philosophers often focus the Other Minds problem very narrowly by asking how I can know, for instance, that my neighbour is in pain. Social scientists are more catholic, addressing themselves to other cultures (with thanks to the long-suffering Azande), to other ages (blessed be the European witch craze) or to particular facets (two cheers for democracy and the enigmatic voter). But the problem is the same, penny plain being the pure version of twopence coloured. It is an epistemological puzzle raised by all the previous chapters, in that all understanding of action involves interpretation and there is always a rival interpretation. Can we ever be sure that the cap fits or that the actor was actually wearing it? Why are all interpretations not equally good?

If action is the rational expression of intention within rules, it has inner determinants of its right interpretation. Without wishing to beg the question against behaviourism, I presume that the inner determinants can in general be known only to an Enquirer who understands the actor's language. This applies even where the Enquirer is the actor but let us separate them. The Other Minds problem is solved, when the Enquirer knows he has understood enough of the Other Mind's statements of experience and belief. How many is enough? I shall argue that he must have enough to distinguish true from false in some cases and to judge what true and false statements the Other Mind would make on other occasions. In other words judgements of truth and falsity and then of rationality and irrationality are the key to knowledge of semantic and syntactic rules. If this can be shown, we can use the understanding of language as a study in the understanding of belief and action, without discussing technical questions of syntax and semantics. I shall claim that the ground of such judgements is *a priori*.

Although loitering with rationalist intent, I do not at all deny that there are empirical questions of interpretation. The conventions of courtly love, the meaning of Hopkins' poetry, the rules of cricket in the Trobriand Islands, the thoughts of Napoleon before Borodino, the principal parts of Latin verbs are not to be settled *a priori*. But there are always *a priori* considerations. That the Enquirer makes discoveries is no more evidence that he starts with a blank notebook than is infant ignorance of the law of non-contradiction evidence that the mind begins as a *tabula rasa*. Empirical questions have to be licensed as empirical, I shall submit, and the validity of licences is always *a priori*. This is a general thesis, holding as much within one culture as among many and within a single language as between two. The problem of categories in interpretation is not solved by recruiting a bilingual. Bilinguals are not magicians. They have solved two empirical problems where the parochial struggle with one; but each empirical solution presupposes a solution to the same *a priori* component of the teaser that there is always another interpretation.

Yet, since it makes no odds how we pose the problem, let us do it for two cultures and languages without bilinguals. That will stop the Enquirer just assuming what I am trying to prove. We send him out with an apparently empty notebook and tell him to fill it with an account of all that is believed, said and done by some unknown people. His generic puzzle is to tell an interesting fact from a bad translation. If he returns with the news that Plato defined justice as a harmony of three organs in the state or that some Germans believe the elk to have no joints in its knees, are we to believe him? Or are we to doubt his translation of δικαιοσυνη and wonder whether, like Caesar, he has had his leg pulled? These are matters for empirical judgement but they become so, I allege, only after the Enquirer has imputed the right degree of the right sort of rationality. That he proceeds on assumptions is uncontentious; that they are rationality assumptions and guaranteed *a priori* is less easy to maintain.[1]

To understand utterances in an unknown tongue, the Enquirer must relate them to one another and to the world. Since relating $x$ to $y$ does not let him translate $x$, unless he can already translate $y$, he must in any case relate some to the world. To gain a bridgehead, by which I mean definitive interpretations of enough terms to restrict possible renderings of others, he needs a set of utterances whose empirical conditions of use he can specify. Hence he must assume that the Other Mind perceives very much what he perceives and says about it very much what he would say. For his only access to the phenomena of the Other Mind's experience is through interpreting behaviour and utterance. If he had to get at the phenomena before he could interpret and had to interpret before he could get at the phenomena, there would be no way in to the circle. He assumes there is a single world being described in two languages, less because there is than because there will have to be. On any other assumption he cannot begin at all.

The nub is that $x$ in one language means the same as $y$ in another (and a man uttering $x$ means the same as a man uttering $y$), only if the conditions for $x$ meaning what it does (or for a man meaning $x$) are satisfied by $y$ (or by a man meaning $y$). In asserting $x$ a man gives his hearers to understand that $x$ is true (distancing uses like sarcasm not being straightforward cases of asserting $x$). To equate $x$ with $y$ at the bridgehead, the Enquirer must take both not merely to be asserted as true but actually to be true. For, although the Other Mind may be asserting falsely that the cow is in the corn, the Enquirer has to understand much before he can find that out. At later stages he can choose whether to interpret $y$ so as to bring it out true or false and with reference to whether he thinks the Other Mind believed it true or false. But the choice

---

[1] The first half of the chapter draws on my papers 'Reason and Ritual', *Philosophy*, 1968 and 'The Limits of Irrationality', *European Journal of Sociology*, 1967, both reprinted in B. Wilson, ed., *Rationality*, Blackwell, 1971 and the former also in A. Ryan, ed., *The Philosophy of Social Explanation*, Oxford, 1973. I remain indebted to Steven Lukes' paper 'Understanding and Explaining Beliefs', *European Journal of Sociology*, 1967, reprinted in Wilson.

is arbitrary, unless he already has a bridgehead. To begin he must find a $y$ whose assertion he can take as the deliberate assertion of a truth.

There are both empirical and *a priori* elements to the flexible mapping of one language onto another. It is empirical that $x$ is to be paired with $y$ rather than with $z$, that a shake of the head means 'No', that the Other Mind has a word for 'cow', indeed that he has a language at all. It is also empirical up to a point how the Other Mind does in fact perceive and conceive his world – the philosopher has no call to quarrel with the detail of a Whorfian hypothesis,[2] which has the speaker of a language discriminate among phenomena according to the categories he has been trained to use. Consequently the bridgehead has something in common with a straightforward hypothesis, in that it can be revised a bit at a time in the light of what comes later. But there are wholly crucial limits to flexibility. There must be a balance of advantage in favour of later revisions and radical revision would destroy the balance. Less cryptically, if the Enquirer starts from $x = y$ and later proposes $x = z$ instead, he must still be guided by having used $x = y$ to establish the meaning of $z$. Similarly a proposal that *gavagai* be translated not as 'rabbit' but as 'four dimensional rabbit-slice' and that all names of concrete particulars be taken in the same sort of way would have to be a proposal for revision of the Enquirer's language too. A Whorfian hypothesis is useful in detail only if it is false in sum, since it destroys in sum the access to the relations it suggests in detail. The Enquirer can, of course, be so flexible that there is no reason to prefer any translation to any other. But, while he hopes to retain any balance of advantage, he must not revise the principles the bridgehead depends on.

What are these principles? They are those of *zweckrational* action applied to the use of language, the link being in the criteria for rational belief. Broadly they amount to an assumption that where the Enquirer believes $P$ on grounds available to the Other Mind, the Other Mind also believes $P$. But there is much unpacking to be done. The grounds I want to consider

---

[2] For Whorf's own account see B. L. Whorf, *Language, Thought and Reality*, ed. J. B. Carroll, MIT Press, 1956.

are observation, evidence, proof and intuition and I stress that they concern the attribution of belief only for securing a bridgehead. Once that is done, the Enquirer can tolerate – and should expect – divergence from his own beliefs; but he can begin only with accord. It is rational to believe $P$ if (but not only if) $P$ describes an observed or intuited state of affairs or is entailed or well evidenced by some proposition which does. For observation the point, as just noted, is not that the same plain facts stare everyone in the face, but that the Enquirer has to assume an overlap, since, where everything is a hypothesis, nothing could count as evidence. Similar points attend the other grounds.

The notions of proof and evidence involve rules for relating propositions. For instance, if $P$ implies $Q$ and $Q$ implies $R$, then *not-R* implies *not-P*. It will be granted, I think, that the Other Mind is impenetrable (or perhaps lacking all cognitive states), unless his beliefs are related somehow. But it is sometimes supposed that the relations may be radically different from ours or (which comes to the same thing) are to be established empirically. Thus, presumably, the Other Mind might have a rule expressed in propositional form by the inference '$\Box (((P{\rightarrow}Q) \& \sim Q) \rightarrow \vdash P)$', which serves the same function as the inference we express by '$\Box(((P{\rightarrow}Q) \& \sim Q) \rightarrow \sim P)$', but, in some sense, conflicts with it. In plainer English, the so-called laws of thought being only the rules we happen to have, it is possible that other minds think and organise belief by different laws. Were this truly possible, the implications would be startling.

Luckily for social theory, the supposition cannot be intelligibly stated. It requires that the Enquirer, faced with the expression '$\Box (((P{\rightarrow}Q) \& \sim Q) \rightarrow \vdash P)$', already have firm grounds for reading '$\Box$' as 'Necessarily', '$\rightarrow$' as 'if . . . then', '$\&$' as 'and', '$\sim$' as 'not', $P$ and $Q$ as variables with constant sense, the brackets as indicators of scope and the whole as a valid formula. He is hesitating only over how to read '$\vdash$', which he has some grounds for taking as 'therefore'. At first sight he can, thus showing that whereas we use $L_1$, where this is an invalid formula, the Other Mind uses $L_2$, where it is valid. But, on reflection, to do so would destroy at least one of his previous identifications. Consider, for example, his identification of '∼' in $L_2$, with '∼' in $L_1$ as an expression of the English word 'not'. A condition for '∼' expressing 'not' is that it is impossible to change the truth while preserving the sense of an expression by substituting 'not' for '∼'. Whatever else '∼' means in $L_2$ it is evidently not what the Enquirer means by 'not'; or, if it is, then at least one other term has been misidentified. The translation of each element singly is a hypothesis to be discarded when the incoherence results. But the test is incoherence and so what is true of each singly is not true of all at once. The global hypothesis at stake is not that the Other Mind has an alternative logic but that he has a logic at all. It is a hypothesis which any success in translation confirms all too completely, since that is precisely the very mark of success.

This argument threatens to prove too much. It threatens to prove that there is only one possible system of logic, to the surprise of logicians, who happily use several. The law of the excluded middle, for instance, which rules that every proposition is either true or false, once belonged among the Laws of Thought but is now often treated as optional or even false. Yet the sort of argument just given seems to imply that 'or' in $L_2$ can be equated with the Enquirer's 'or' only if $L_2$ includes the law of the excluded middle. Indeed it threatens to prove in general that $x$ never means the same as $y$, since $y$ is never fully intersubstitutable with $x$ and so always breaks some condition for $x$ meaning what it does. But these runaway results follow, only if we treat the criteria for accepting or rejecting possible translations as part of what is to be discovered by translation. The Enquirer must impute consistency and so must be able to take the rules of consistency as given. The rules are, I think, a gloss on the proposition that the implications of a true statement are true, a gloss sufficiently specified by three rules –

(1) The law of identity (If $P$, then $P$)
(2) The law of non–contradiction (Not-($P$ and $not$-$P$))
(3) *Modus Ponens* (If ($P$ and (if $P$, then $Q$)) then $Q$)

Equally the translation of $x$ by $y$ on an occasion of utterance does not require that $x$ and $y$ be intersubstitutable on all possible occasions. It requires only that $x$ is better translated on that occasion by $y$ than by any $z$ and the point of the argument is again that the criteria of semantic equivalence need to be given in advance. If they are part of the project, the project becomes impossible, since there are then no rules to conduct it by. English and Navajo can have different semantic rules but not different functions served by their semantic rules or different criteria for what relation holds among equivalent expressions.

In imputing consistency the Enquirer is also imputing the intuition needed to grasp logical relations. For knowing that $P$ implies $Q$ is not solely a matter of being able to follow a rigmarole which starts with $P$ and ends with $Q$. The point of the rigmarole is to lead the mind's eye to see that (If $P$, then $Q$) is a necessary truth. The clearest example is perhaps the three logical truths in the last paragraph, since they are presupposed by all proof and must be grasped prior to any proof of them. But in general necessary truths are not true because they are provable but provable because they are true. Proof is a reason for belief but not a ground of truth. A proof of $Q$ from $P$, which gives conditional knowledge that $Q$, also gives unconditional knowledge that, if $P$, then $Q$. There is also more to it, since a proof of $Q$ from $P$ gives reason to believe $Q$ true, only if there is reason to believe $P$ true; and to believe $Q$ necessarily true, only if there is reason to believe $P$ necessarily true.[3] So, in imputing consistency, the Enquirer imputes rational belief in unproved premises and necessary truths, in parallel with belief in facts of observation which need no evidence. He imputes the intuition needed to grasp what follows from what and so is accepting or rejecting possible interpretations according to whether he would himself judge the results consistent. He can attribute inconsistent beliefs only after he has successfully imputed consistent ones.

This is a contentious way of looking at logical relations and at knowledge of necessary truths and I include it here partly as a foretaste of what will be said about *Verstehen* and ideal types. It may strengthen the point to apply it to the notion of evi-

---

[3] I am ignoring as irrelevant the proof of $Q$ by *reductio ad absurdum* from an assumption of *not-Q*.

dence. The Other Mind does not believe only what he observes, intuits or formally deduces. When he rationally believes, say, that rain is coming, he does so on evidence. Schematically, he believes $Q$ for the reason that he believes $P$, where $P$ does not entail $Q$. $Q$ asserts that something was, will be, is always, would be or would have been the case. $Q$ is then rationally held only if there is a connectedness to experience which logic does not capture and $P$ is no reason for believing $Q$, unless $P$ stands to $Q$ in this relation. Once again the Enquirer cannot discover what the relation is, since he needs to know what it is before he can identify $Q$. He therefore imputes his own notion of evidence and his justification can only be that it is *the* notion of evidence. Admittedly the library shelves are full of books offering rival canons of evidence, just as they are of books supporting rival theories of logic. But they are all theories of *evidence* and the librarian has rightly shelved them together, including those in other languages. No doubt the Enquirer imputes the minimal notion but he cannot avoid imputing any.

There are, I daresay, other relations too. Language is used to convey ritual, sacred, aesthetic or mystic thought and experience. Metaphors, images and gestures to a hidden reality are as much a part of science as of everyday life. It is far from plain that the web of rational belief can be woven from proof and evidence alone. But we have enough to work with.[4] I have tried to show that the Enquirer must impute before he can discover, since in interpreting it is not enough just to pay attention. He must also judge. He says to himself, 'I assume the Other Mind to be a rational man. I take it that his beliefs are, on the whole, rationally connected and that, usually, his utterances express his beliefs. I take it that he uses words as tokens governed by the rules for their type and that literal sense informs the stock from which the richest patterns are wrought. I take it that he seeks to make himself understood, recognising that verbal arabesques are mere sound, if they destroy the sense of the stock. So, when I hit on an apparent translation which would show him not to be a rational man

---

[4] The issue is taken further in 'Reason and Ritual', *loc. cit.*

*überhaupt*, I reject the translation. Language is not a mere vehicle or device, a set of external rules for generating well-formed strings of words. It is a way of uttering thoughts, with the intention of being understood. To grasp the rules, I must grasp the thoughts; to grasp the thoughts, I must grasp the rules; I can break the circle only by imputing rationality.'

The rational man, then, speaks enough of the truth to be understood. But he does not speak only the truth. On occasion he may say what is false, believing it to be true, say what is false, believing it to be false, or make assertions whose truth cannot be judged. He may also say what is fitting, expected, amusing, shocking, absurd, inspiring or misleading. He may utter out of love, embarrassment, fear or malice. If he said only what was true because he knew it to be true, he would say very little. The three cases to consider are the rational but untrue, the irrational and the non-rational.

The Enquirer has some latitude with these categories but his best direct defence of an interpretation is that it makes the Other Mind more rational than its rivals do. By way of illustration consider the problem of reconstructing the text of a Latin poet from conflicting manuscripts. According to that scourge of editors A. E. Housman, it is the mark of a poor scholar to pick out an authoritative manuscript and then loll on it. Thus, faced with four MSS, *a*, *b*, *c* and *d*, the editor might make it his rule to follow *a* wherever possible and reject it only where its readings are patently erroneous. Housman will have none of this sloth:

Either *a* is the source of *b* and *c* and *d* or it is not. If it is, then never in any case should recourse be had to *b* or *c* or *d*. If it is not, then the rule is irrational; for it involves the assumption that wherever *a*'s scribes made a mistake they produced an impossible reading. Three minutes' thought would suffice to find this out; but thought is irksome and three minutes a long time.[5]

There is no way of knowing that *a* is authoritative, he continues, without judging its readings to be right. Nor is decid-

---

[5] From the preface to his edition of Juvenal, *D. Iunii Iuvenalis Saturae*, reprinted Cambridge, 1956. Lovers of invective will be no less taken with the preface to his edition of Manilius, *M. Manilii Astronomicon Liber Primus*, reprinted Cambridge, 1937, and *Liber Quintus*, London, 1930. The latter is referred to in my next paragraph.

ing to follow *a* at all costs an alternative to judging. It is merely pre-empting the hope of good judgement by a global bad judgement.

That is all very well; but how is a virtuous editor to judge a right reading? In the preface to Manilius Book v Housman bids him 'read attentively, think correctly, omit no relevant consideration and repress self-will' and to bring to the task 'just literary perception, congenial intimacy with the author, experience which must have been won by study and mother wit which he must have brought from his mother's womb'. Students of criticism will recognise the questions raised or begged. But the question for us is what is meant by a right reading. Housman speaks elsewhere of readings being 'intrinsically probable' and 'intrinsically improbable', a matter judged presumably by experience and mother wit. But the occult process seems designed only for immaculate authors. It might arrive at what the original should have been but bad authors do not write what they should. Had Euclid survived only in corrupt manuscripts, we could probably reconstruct him by wit but we could never do the same for Johnny Smith's school mathematics answers. For that we need a criterion of what is, so to speak, extrinsically probable.

There are several possible ones, no doubt, but the point is that they are secondary. It is the rational use of language which fixes the meaning for the stock and provides the first check on ambiguity. Once the editor has the stock, he can try to infer the author's meaning from the text's meaning; but, starting from scratch, he needs texts where he can infer the text's meaning from what it would be rational for the author to mean by the text. For ill-thought, ill-expressed texts he relies on what other authors have rationally meant before.

Housman was editing poets and might object to describing immaculate poetry as the rational use of language. But then he did not have to start from scratch. For him the Other Minds problem had already reached the empirical stage. Yet even at the empirical stage irrational utterances are to be interpreted by knowing when it would be rational to utter them. As in the last chapter, it will not do to argue that an author always says what seemed to him rational at the time. Subjective rationality is still a passing score on the objective test and not full marks on some subjective test. The pass mark must be high enough to help us decide whether he believes what he seems to say or means what he seems to believe. The more secure the bridgehead, the lower is the score which has to be imputed. Interpretative charity is a virtue in moderation, a vice in excess.

The Other Mind, then, is to be made rational, where possible, irrational, where necessary, and never non-rational at all. Belief, utterance and action can be identified, only if there is some good or bad reason for them. Thereby hangs a long tale for another occasion but its moral will be that the 'traditional' or 'expressive' (or whatever is used by contrast with the instrumental) is also rational or irrational. I drew the moral before when arguing that *Zweckrationalität* is neither the only nor even the primary kind and I lack the space and courage to add to it here.

In sum, then, utterances are actions performed with tokens from stock. Provided we are sure of the stock, we ask the meaning of a token before asking whether it was rationally uttered. But, where the stock is in doubt, the relation is the other way. If the utterance seems outrageous, there is an automatic case for finding it another meaning; which goes to show that we do credit the utterer with reasons, even when we do not trouble to ask what they are. If the utterance is part of the Enquirer's bridgehead, rationality and meaning go together. He constructs his bridgehead from assertive utterances expressing true and rational beliefs, assuming the Other Mind to be a rational man by *the* criteria of rationality. Since the assumption regulates his findings, every finding is bound to confirm it. So it is not an empirical hypothesis, tested against experience, but a precondition *a priori* of the possibility of understanding.

There is a broader thesis about the rational and the real here. But, before picking it out, I want to extend the argument from the identification of belief expressed in language to the explanation of belief in general. It is often said that we can and should explain the holding of beliefs without judging their truth or rationality. Examples might be accounting for religious affiliation by social class or for consumption patterns by

155

advertising directed to psychological traits. Sociologists of knowledge are prone to this view, if they are arrogant enough to be sure that belief is always caused by social structures or humble enough to deny the enquirer all right to judge others. In the next pages I shall try to show that explanation always involves judgement, starting with a schematic exercise in the sociology of knowledge.

If there is a global problem of Other Minds, it applies to discovering what sociologists believe and why. Since they do not all share the same beliefs, let us divide them, very much for the sake of argument, into two exclusive and exhaustive groups, by the litmus test of whether they hold some central tenet. The tenet could be left blank – call it '$P$' – and that would save offence. But I shall risk giving it a crude content, strictly for epistemological purposes. So let us suppose the crux is whether social structures, normative and non-normative, are the work of rational agents or whether, on the contrary, action and belief are always to be explained as the product of social structures. All sociologists must subscribe to one of these beliefs and no compromise is allowed. I ask everyone to enter into the spirit of the game.

Now let us imagine three sociologists, Hook, Line and Sinker. Hook is doing research into the beliefs of sociologists; Line believes structures to be the work of rational agents; Sinker believes that structures explain action and belief. *Ex hypothesei* Hook agrees with one or other of them and there will be four phases. Firstly Hook, agreeing with Sinker, investigates Line. Secondly, still agreeing with Sinker, he investigates Sinker. Thirdly, switching to Line's point of view, he investigates Sinker again. Fourthly, still siding with Line, he investigates Line. Each phase will pave the way for the final part of the chapter.

Firstly, then, Hook sets about Line, on the assumption that Line's beliefs have structural determinants. He describes Line's world from Line's point of view, including Line's own beliefs about how it works, with whatever measure of interpretive charity is needed to yield an account which makes sense to Line. Then he describes this same world again in some functionalist terms, for instance those which place Line in a homeostatic context of external institutions. Finally, using the latter to explain the former, he shows what beliefs it would be functional for a man in Line's position to hold and accounts for discrepancies either *ad hoc* or by tensions in the external structures. If the results are compact and of high predictive power, he cites this fact as empirical evidence for his original assumption that structure determines belief.

The programme involves judging the truth and rationality of at least some of Line's beliefs. In particular Line's beliefs about the direction of explanation and the nature of social action contradict Hook's. Were Line right, Hook's research would rest on so large an error that all its explanatory findings would be wrong. So here is one set of beliefs which Hook must judge and reject. He cannot maintain blandly that their truth is irrelevant to their explanation. Nor can he cover himself by saying that their rationality matters but their truth does not. For, if Line has objectively good reasons for believing that explanation runs the other way, then Hook should accept them too; and, as argued before, subjective rationality is to be taken as derivative from objective. Nor can Hook suspend judgement on the pragmatic ground that his own approach is fertile rather than well-evidenced. For, in so far as he is using it at all, he is to that extent betting against Line's beliefs. There is no neutral position.

Once neutrality is breached, the pace quickens. It is not only Line's explicit beliefs about sociological method which conflict with Hook's. Any belief will do, which implies that Hook's explanation of why it is held is wrong. If Line were a Freudian, an existentialist or, indeed, anything but Hook's brand of structuralist, Hook would have to pass judgement. Nor need the conflicting opinions be academic. Were Line a disciple of Samuel Smiles or a capitalist with a Protestant ethic, who believed that he had taken to commerce on divine advice, he would hold beliefs whose truth would entail the falsity of Hook's explanation. Actors in every age and culture explain their beliefs to themselves and Hook admitted as much when he started by describing Line's world from within. Whenever the truth of Hook's explanation implies the falsity of the beliefs it explains, Hook cannot avoid judgement.

Hook is deep in ontology. To propose a method of explanation is to claim that the world works by the method. If structuralism is true, then God does not prompt Calvinists to industrial enterprise through the small voice of conscience. A method for detecting causal laws commits the user to a world which contains them. If Hook chooses his methods pragmatically or relies on several, then he either asserts that there really are several sorts of connection or, as a merely tentative ontologist, must settle for equally tentative explanations. In general, the Enquirer, no less than the Other Mind, tries to make the world intelligible to himself. In the action of explaining, he is asserting a metaphysic. Call it 'P', including:

$P_1$: methodological propositions about the criteria of explanation

$P_2$: theoretical propositions about the sort of sociological explanations which satisfy $P_1$

$P_3$: ontological propositions implied or presupposed by $P_2$

$P_4$: epistemological propositions justifying $P_1$

$P_5$: ontological propositions implied or presupposed by $P_4$

He is committed to rejecting any of the Other Mind's beliefs which conflict with any implication of $P$. In plainer speech, he tackles his victim armed with a method of enquiry, a set of sociological concepts, a model of man and of society, a theory of knowledge and a cosmology. His every explanation is therefore a judgement on the victim's own view of the world.

Secondly Hook, still believing that structure explains belief, investigates Sinker, who takes the same view. For the previous reasons, Hook must judge Sinker's beliefs, this time pronouncing them true and rational. But now there is a delicious snag. Why does Sinker believe that structure explains belief? The Sinkers of my acquaintance all give intellectual, epistemically-charged reasons. So did Hook a moment ago, when we had him cite his findings as empirical evidence for the worth of his approach. But these are examples of the sort of beliefs which Hook is committed to rejecting. He need not reject them as mere rationalisations or epiphenomena, since he can allow that beliefs may be immediately caused by other beliefs. Moreover he can treat beliefs as having important effects in masking and perpetuating social systems, after the manner of materialist theories of ideology. But he cannot stop there. It is not in his book to grant that any belief is held or any action done solely or finally because there is good reason for it. Structure explains belief. So Sinker's good reasons must finally be Sinker's 'good' reasons, reasons which satisfy criteria whose authority is finally the mere stamp of some socially significant body. By all means let Hook and Sinker explain why they believe that structure explains belief by appealing at first to the rules of the Logicians' Union and the Sociologists' Guild. But let them not forget to add a causal explanation of the power of these bodies and of why they endorse those particular rules. Even if reasons are causes, they also have causes – otherwise structures are no longer trumps and Hook cannot take all the tricks.

Hook is now in an impossible position. If he follows this advice, he destroys his earlier explanation of Line's beliefs. He earlier judged Line's beliefs false and Line's reasons for holding them bad reasons. He was not trying to convict Line of heresy by the prevailing norms of the Logicians' Union and Sociologists' Guild. Nor would he have succeeded, since the Union is neutral between consistent sociological theories and the Guild divided. What he believed and needed to say was that Line was in error. Structuralism, he insists, has reason on its side or, insofar as reason is certified by some body, the body has good reason for its certificates. There can be no structural explanation for his holding the belief that every other belief has a structural explanation, unless this crucial belief is false. He cannot afford to try for all the tricks.

When are structural explanations of belief not trumps? The exception just made can only be a general one for any free-floating intelligence to justify the holding of a belief by showing it true and rational. In other words intelligence is *freischwebend* whenever it holds true beliefs for good reasons. In the last chapter we met a man who took an umbrella because it was, he knew, likely to rain and because an umbrella was, he knew, the best way to keep dry and because it was, he knew, against his interests to get wet. Where or in so far as these conditions did not hold, there was scope for causal explanation by reference to the *Regenschirmerei* of the British um-class. In so far as they did, there was no more to be said. There would be further questions – why he owned an umbrella or why it had a gold handle – but they would be premised on recognising that he had solved the problem set by the weather. Similarly the historian can ask why Babylonian mathematics were ahead of Etruscan at the same date and show how the Babylonian social system helped what the Etruscan hindered; but he cannot sensibly ask why they were different, until he knows how they differed. Crucially the Babylonians *knew more* than the Etruscans, as any history of mathematics makes clear. Hook's exception in his own case reinforces what was said before. To make the exception is to recognise an ideal type of self-sufficient explanation.

The moral is now wider. Hook must judge the believer's reasons for every belief and action to be explained. There is no structural explanation for what is its own explanation. I do not mean that there is a sociology only of ignorance, since it remains worth finding out what social conditions further the spread of knowledge. Also we often cannot judge where reason lies and must bet that the believer does not know either. But we must always start laying our bets, since the type and mixture of explanations depends on them. Hence there is a moral too for the study of ideologies, which can now be assigned to a superstructure and explained as products of a socio-economic base, only insofar as they are false. True consciousness is its own explanation.

For the third and fourth phases, Hook changes horses and starts again. He still treats social and intellectual systems as distinct but reverses the direction of explanation. Like Line, he believes that men construct the social world and that men are essentially rational agents. Sinker still believes that social systems are always external, constraining and the source of explanations of the last resort.

Sinker now presents a fresh target. Why does he hold these mistaken beliefs? No doubt he has some reasons, enough to let Hook be sure that he does indeed hold the beliefs, thus partly explaining them and partly picking out what needs a causal explanation. For the rest Hook must produce a strong actionist's theory of error. Broadly, Sinker is in a state of false consciousness, deceived by others or self-deceived. Perhaps he belongs to a sociology department, whose members feel powerless to influence the rational–legal structure of their university. They have either inherited their serfdom from long-dead professors or conveniently forgotten that they invented the structure themselves a few years back. (This is roughly the difference between old and new universities.) In either case Hook is accusing Sinker of some degree of bad faith. Admittedly the deception may be highly convincing. Dead professors and selves can truly be external and constraining; what a group could do, if it united, may be impossible for one member alone or for a sub-group. But Hook is now a strong actionist and so must insist that somewhere there is a more autonomous and powerful Prospero who constructed the enmeshing social reality. He must insist also that the spell can be broken. So Sinker is a fool or a rogue – a fool who cannot see behind the scenario or a rogue who prefers not to look. Breaking the spell need not be easy and may require collective action but the point is that it is possible. To explain why what is is involves explaining why what could have been is not. While Hook was a structuralist, he believed that the spell could not be broken and so did not have to explain why it endured. Now he does and that is why Sinker now presents a fresh target.

The normative, prescriptive, aspect of rational explanation obtrudes further when, lastly, Hook renews his investigation of Line. Both are trying to extend the scope of rational action and Hook hopes to influence Sinker by showing him how to take control but that involves upsetting Sinker's basic assumption, whereas Line already accepts rational belief and action as their own explanation. Yet Hook and Line will not be in total accord. We defined rational action as action done because it is most likely to secure the agent's real interests. The definition can be disputed; it is an old and massive question where the agent's real interests lie; there is fierce debate about how to judge the best means to secure them. As an actionist, Hook does not have to make himself a free-floating exception in order to mount his enquiry but he cannot claim special

161

status. He is party to his own investigation and may find Line's beliefs more rational than his own. With all branches of social science and ethics at stake, each claim to identify some departure from the ideally rational will be contentious. None the less Hook is committed to try. If the type of explanation depends on the rationality of what is to be explained, every belief and every action has to be judged.

Now let us drop the coarse pretence that every sociologist is a Line or a Sinker. The real elements of the exercise were only the conflicting systems of belief. What makes beliefs into a system is the presence of beliefs about beliefs. The web includes purported explanations of its own elements. Some profess a causal determinism, either in sum, as with a convinced causal determinist, or in part, as with a man who self-consciously traces his repressions to something nasty in the woodshed. Others assign purportedly good reasons for holding other beliefs. Where these reasons are objectively sufficient, no further explanation is called for, as is conceded, indeed, by any Enquirer who claims sufficient reason for his own beliefs about the explanation of any beliefs, including his own. Hence to explain a universally held belief is to endorse it; to explain a disputed belief is to back oneself against the Other Mind or one Other Mind against another. Understanding starts with true beliefs rationally held, continues with rational but false beliefs and switches to the passive mode only with the irrational. In both identifying and explaining there are upper and lower limits to the irrational beliefs which can be ascribed to rational men.

Finally there has been the nagging thought throughout that reality is not an observable, independent check on rational belief. The best eyesight will not reveal whether there are witches in Africa nor the best hearing whether the Azande believe there are; the Zande who looks for witches in England will find them prevalent, as a prelude to explaining the British lack of reliable oracles and magic. This is a colourful case of the epistemological thought that experience is never brute but always conceptualised. The puzzle set for understanding language was that there is always another interpretation. It is also the most general epistemological puzzle of all. I shall not offer to solve it but I shall make two points to ward off the evil eye of any malignant demon reading these pages.

The first is that the social sciences are in no evidently worse plight than the natural. The social world might seem peculiarly fragile. Cannot a web of shared meanings and attitudes vanish like Prospero's isle? Are not deviants, unlike elephants, waved into existence with a conceptual wand? If physical objects are known to us as an interpretation of experience, are not minds an interpretation of an interpretation? The questions sound disturbing but nothing follows, when they are unscrambled. Meanings may be gossamer stuff but a true empirical statement of their existence is as true and as empirical as one about mountains. Attitudes are created but so are pyramids. The labelling of someone deviant is a fiat with physical, social and moral consequences but, as when a court finds a defendant negligent, there can be objective grounds for applying labels. Elephants too are a feature of experience picked out with a label and, if the cases are in the end dissimilar, it takes much to prove it. Electrons are also known to us as an interpretation of an interpretation and scientific theory has long wrestled with the problem of unobservables. Admittedly minds are known, I have claimed, with special aid from rationality assumptions and the explanation of action is peculiar. But we have yet to find a special problem of objectivity. I do not care to rule one out but at least it is not evidently there and it is a puzzle for all sciences that there is always another interpretation.

Secondly, there is a historical reason why the puzzle is so acute at present. We tend to start in innocence from the idea that what it is rational to believe about the world is bounded by the objective facts on the side of experience and, on the side of conjecture, by the truths of logic, mathematics and other objective *a priori* systems; between the actual and the impossible lies an objective realm of probability and statistics. This comfortable view has been shaken for us by Logical Positivism and Conceptual Pragmatism. The former weakened the *a priori* bound by treating necessary truths as analytic statements guaranteed only by linguistic rules which men can make and unmake. The latter has weakened the other bound by denying the independence of facts for reasons sketched in chapter 3. Epistemologists are therefore open to heady thoughts from hermeneutics and the sociology of knowledge which challenge old ways to objectivity. The demon of doubt is not content but he is much enlivened. I do not offer to scotch him and these glib remarks are not born of conceit that I know the truth. But a rationalist line does have one promising advantage. If Logical Positivism is claimed to be a set of epistemological truths, it falls foul of its own analytic–synthetic distinction. If Conceptual Pragmatism itself can be rationally revised, it is false; and, if it cannot be rationally revised, it is again false. But there is nothing to embarrass rationalists in the supposition that rationalism is true.

'Rationalism' continues to have three senses. The blandest is that there is enough order in the world of experience for science to be possible. Yet perception gives us no (or too little) unvarnished news and the riddle of induction remains inscrutable. So, if we are to know that science is possible, we shall have to know *a priori*. What the world must be like, if we are to explain its workings, and that the world is in truth ordered on the principles we are bound to assume are topics for rationalist metaphysics in the grand manner and traditional sense. The social sciences have the same need for a rational subject matter but also in a further sense, which makes the rational actor the ideal type against which actual departures are measured. Here again, it will be urged in the next chapter, we must know what is rational *a priori* before we can know what is actual. So, if I may mark our advance with an old and enigmatic slogan, it begins to emerge that the rational is the real.

# 8

# Ideal understanding

When lovers commune, they learn what cannot be expressed or known in other ways. Or so it is plausibly said. Donne's poem 'The Extasie' tells how

Our soules, (which to advance their state,
Were gone out,) hung 'twixt her, and mee.
And whilst our soules negotiate there,
We like sepulchrall statues lay;
All day, the same our postures were,
And wee said nothing all the day.

A behaviourist would have had a thin time of it. Yet negotiate they did, by a process needing a special sort of *Verstehen*. The sharpest observer cannot understand, unless he were

so by love refin'd,
That he soules language understood
And by good love were grown all minde.

I do not doubt that there is a process by which not only lovers empathise. Indeed I would gladly present an epistemology for it, if I could see my way to a pure science of ecstasy. But for present purposes nothing less would do. If the insights can be expressed and known in other ways, then empathy becomes, in principle, merely a short cut. To put it more sonorously, where the usual canons of validation apply, *Verstehen* is only a heuristic device. The skills of anthropologists in the field, art critics, personnel managers and participant observers in general are not our concern and this chapter is not about empathy.

It is about knowledge of the rational thing to do or the *a priori* understanding of necessities to which rational action is subject. The crux will be that rational action is a skill, needing knowledge and power. When it is exercised, the actor could have done otherwise but could not have done better. That $x$ was the rational thing to do is, if true, a necessary truth, knowable both *a posteriori* and *a priori*. Irrational action is a failure to find the best move and its explanation depends on knowing what the best move would have been. These cryptic ideas will first be deployed with the aid of chess and Kriegspiel, where the distinction between *a posteriori* and *a priori* comes out instructively and the skill depends on anticipating an as yet undiscovered theory of the game. (I apologise to those who cannot tell a Dutch Defence from a Guico Piano and promise that they will not have to.) Then there will be a section on the kind of necessity at issue, with a plea for the old idea that sound theory rests on *real* definitions of its essential concepts. Next the point will be pressed with a fresh example, that of Steven Lukes' reflections on Power, which make sense, I allege, only as an attempt at a real definition. The chapter will end with a word about models in economics and sociology and with a general moral for the use of ideal types in explanation.

In chess an ideal measure of rational play is needed for understanding what it would actually be rational to play; in Kriegspiel the ideal is also needed to identify the actual move played. These points need more than a sentence apiece, however, and I hope to be forgiven an excursion into this arcane world. The grandmaster, after an hour's thought, advances his king's pawn one square. Why? The question might be why he played the move or why the move was the one to play. The answer might be the same but it need not be, since even grandmasters nod. So let us start by asking what sort of knowledge a man has when he knows that P–K6 is the best move. It may be uncontentiously *a priori* knowledge. In some positions there is one demonstrably best move. Necessarily, given the rules and object of the game, in this position only P–K6 secures a win (or saves a loss). In the clearest case the player (call him White) can, for any black defence, point to a series of moves which end in checkmate. Which series will actually occur depends on what black plays. Indeed none need occur, if White makes an error or drops dead. But it is still

necessarily true that White has a won game and can be known
*a priori* to be true. Slightly less clear is the case where P–K6
gains only what should be a decisive advantage. For instance if
White is a knight up and P–K6 blocks Black's best hope of
counterplay, the game is 'won with best play', and a strong
player could rationally expect to win it, perhaps without
knowing quite how. Although it would take too much com-
puter time to analyse all variations, it could in principle be
done and would prove it in White's power to mate. There are
degrees of rational expectation here, depending on the size of
White's advantage and how precisely he can specify his
strategy, but he does often know that he has a won game.
When it is true, then it is necessarily true. Philosophers will
agree, I think, that it is an analytic truth and, I venture to add
from the end of chapter 3, one in which concepts of chess, as
well as of logic, occur essentially.

A won game remains necessarily a won game, however
hard it is to spot the win. But in murkier positions rational
expectation no longer amounts to *a priori* knowledge. White, a
knight up but with some compensating weakness, may none
the less still chalk up the win in his mind. In the absence of any
proof, what could give him the right to be sure? He gets it not
because most strong players do win from similar positions but
because he has a sound theory for assessing advantage in chess
(and, incidentally, for deciding which positions are similar).
Previously it was enough to work out the logic of the rules as it
applied to his particular position. Now he needs to know why
his position is of a sort likely to turn into a clear case with best
play. Why, for example, are two bishops usually worth more
than two knights, although one knight is usually the equal of
one bishop? Typically he invokes concepts like 'force', 'space'
and 'time'. Force might be a measure of the overall compara-
tive ratings of pieces, counting queen as 9, castle as 5, knight or
bishop as 3 and pawn as 1. Space might refer to the number of
squares which he can occupy with impunity or which his
opponent cannot. Time might be a matter of the speed with
which force can bear on a given target. There are rival theories
of advantage in chess and I do not insist that these are the right
concepts to use. Epistemologically, however, I do insist that

the analysis of positions requires a theory using concepts of chess not found in the rule book but justified by their success as an aid to winning. In each position White stands necessarily superior or necessarily equal to or necessarily inferior to Black. A theory of chess shows why this is so, in a way which lets us know which relation actually holds. It both justifies a claim to know and shows how to proceed. It also explains why strong players do win from similar positions, having explained what counts as a similar position.

There has been no whiff of contingency so far about the best move itself. It is contingent that White has a position where P–K6 is the best move; but not contingent that P–K6 is the best move in that position. It is contingent that chess is no longer played under medieval rules; but not contingent that under modern rules P–K6 is best in that position. It is contingent that White is trying to win rather than to inflate Black's ego; but not contingent that, to win under modern rules from that position, P–K6 is the best move. It is not true that, if the cow is in the corn, then necessarily it is in the corn; whereas, unelliptically stated, if P–K6 is the best move, then necessarily it is the best move. It does not follow that knowledge of its merit is always *a priori* knowledge but there is nothing contingent about the truth itself.

Chess always seems too narrow a model of social action, for reasons some of which can be brought out, without conceding much to human warmth, by considering Kriegspiel. Kriegspiel is the fiendish version of chess where each player has a separate board and is not told what his opponent has moved. He gleans what meagre clues he can from an umpire, who has the only complete picture. Thus White, at his turn, knows his own position definitively but places any black pieces on his board at his own risk of error. If he proposes an illegal move, the umpire will forbid it. If he captures, the umpire will announce the square but not the pieces involved. If he gives check, the umpire says, 'Check' and tells Black the direction he is checked from. Other rules are as in mere chess. It may sound as if Kriegspiel can be played only by guess or by God; but in fact it is a game of such skill that the German army has used it to train staff officers for battle.

The special skill lies in inferring the opponent's likeliest positions (keeping several in mind at once) and in misleading him. It rests on a little information and more assumption. White knows that Black is obeying the rules of chess and what there is to be learnt from the umpire's announcements and prohibitions. He assumes that Black has some degree of skill both at chess and, importantly, at Kriegspiel. It is crucial what degree he assumes, under- and overestimates being equally expensive. He can adjust the degree assumed, as the game progresses, provided he bears in mind that Black is trying to mislead him. It is worth noting that there is no one most rational opening in chess and so no question of perfect information could arise in Kriegspiel, even if Black carelessly played chess instead of Kriegspiel. Finally a general skill at chess is also needed.

The better player at Kriegspiel has the shrewder idea of the likely whole position. He infers his opponent's likely moves by calculating first what the best move would be and then how likely his opponent is to have played it. Why go this long way round? Why not simply infer what his opponent was likely to play? Is it not often positively unlikely that the best move was played? Well, the best move at Kriegspiel is not to be confused with the best move at chess. The umpire may know, for instance, that White can mate in three moves; but it may not be rational for White to play the first of them, since he may have little reason to suspect the mate and good reason to think the move likely to cost him his queen. What the chess player sees the Kriegspieler infers, partly by knowing how strong his opponent is. He has to understand the standard, if he is to know how high the opponent scores on it. Also he must adjust his play to the strength of the other. A move which would outwit an expert might lose to a rabbit, just as a double bluff may fail against a fool. The skill lies in using the clues as evidence not only of the last move but also of the opponent's general skill. The Kriegspieler cannot play the board well without playing the man; to play the man he must take his measure.

Here, then, explaining why a move was actually made comes into explaining how best to answer it. The same is occasionally true in chess too. For example White may play an inferior move on purpose in a drawn-looking position, for the sake of complexities. Or, faced with a long defence of a slightly worse position, he may prefer a double-edged move to tempt Black into overreaching himself. These are rational tactics only if White knows his man. He must gauge Black's strength and also his temperament, if the bait is not to be scorned and the strategic error punished. Strength is a matter of how well he plays, temperament of why he favours some types of move over others. In winning positions at chess the soundest move is always best and it does not matter what Black is thinking. In drawn or losing positions it may be more rational to play the man than the board. At Kriegspiel to play the board one must play the man, since the man is the best clue to the board. In all these cases the ideally rational is the guide to understanding the position and what best to play in it.

Even at Kriegspiel, if P–K6 is the best move, it is necessarily the best. The calculation has more premises and more unknowns and there is no crisp established theory for assessing advantage. But truths which we would know *a priori*, if we knew more, do not become contingent, if we know less. Kriegspiel comes closer to social life, because uncertainty is endemic but what is rational is still necessarily rational.

Chess yields the thought that an ideal measure of rational play is needed for understanding what it would actually be rational to play. Kriegspiel adds that the ideal is also needed to identify and judge what the actual is. In both games knowing why P–K6 was played depends on knowing how rational a move it was. But, before trying these thoughts further, we need a note on the idea of necessary truth. There is no uncontentious way of distinguishing necessary from contingent – nor even of claiming that there is a distinction to draw – but Leibniz' *Monadology* is a classic starting point –

33. There are also two kinds of truths, those of reasoning and those of fact. Truths of reasoning are necessary and their opposite is impossible, and those of fact are contingent and their opposite is possible. When a truth is necessary, its reason can be found by analysis, resolving it into more simple ideas and truths until we reach those which are primitive.

34. It is thus that mathematicians by analysis reduce speculative theorems and practical canons to definitions, axioms and postulates.

35. And there are finally simple ideas, definitions of which cannot be given; there are also axioms and postulates, in a word, primary principles, which cannot be proved, and indeed need no proof; and these are identical propositions, whose opposite involves an express contradiction.

The reader must look elsewhere for a proper treatment of this vast topic and I shall say enough only to sign-post the line I shall be taking.[1] Those convinced by recent pragmatist assaults on the related analytic-synthetic distinction will be unimpressed.[2] So, ultimately, will any who still uphold that distinction in Positivist spirit;[3] to say nothing of those who view the question outside the frame of traditional epistemology.[4] What follows is a note to be treated with caution but crucial for the rest of the chapter.

Broadly, then, there is a class of truths whose denial is impossible, with at least apparent examples in logic, mathematics, formal systems like kinship algebra or neo-Classical micro-economic theory, and perhaps in epistemology or metaphysics and, arguably at any rate, in ethics and theology. This list is cursory and incomplete, although thinkers who accept any necessary truths usually agree to the first three headings. But it is a mysterious class. For a start, it is no good trying to *define* a necessary truth as one whose denial is impossible, since the sense of 'impossible' here presupposes the original idea of necessity. For, in order to relate '$P$ is necessarily true' by definition to any other expression, we must grasp what is asserted by a function of the form '$X = df Y$' and be able to know that it is truly asserted. The relation involved can be analysed only with the aid of statements of the form under

---

[1] Arthur Pap, *Semantics and Necessary Truth*, Yale UP, 1958 is again my preferred source of wisdom.

[2] The central line remains W. v. O. Quine's 'Two Dogmas of Empiricism' in *From a Logical Point of View*, Harvard University Press, 1961.

[3] A. J. Ayer, *Language, Truth and Logic*, chapter IV is still the most terse and elegant expression of the spirit.

[4] This is not to say that all would be hostile, however much they would complain that the questions must be treated at far greater depth. See, for instance, G. Harman and D. Davidson, eds., *Semantics of Natural Languages*, Reidel Dordrecht, 1971, especially S. Kripke's essay 'Naming and Necessity'.

analysis. So, while it does not matter that 'necessary' be the label given to the concept ultimately presupposed, no advance is possible unless something is presupposed which is equivalent to the concept of necessity. Hence a criterion is the most offered by characterising a necessary truth as one whose denial is impossible.[5]

Also, if there is a point in trying to define a necessary truth in this way, it is to suggest that truths are necessary *because* their denial can be demonstrably reduced *ad absurdum*. The suggestion is to be resisted for reasons given in the previous chapter. Proof reveals truth and is a reason for claiming knowledge; but is not a reason or ground of truth. Also it goes only so far and Leibniz halts at 'definitions, axioms and postulates', or, as he says in paragraph 35, 'in a word, primary principles, which cannot be proved, and indeed need no proof'. (He is on weaker ground in calling them 'identical propositions'.) If they needed proof, we would have no necessary truths. As urged before, a conditional proof of '*Q*' from '*P*' is an unconditional assertion of 'if *P*, then *Q*' or of 'if *A*, then (if *P*, then *Q*)', where '*A*' is whatever is needed for the proof of '*Q*' from '*P*'.

Moreover it is too easy to presume that '*P*' is necessarily true only if '*not–P*' is *logically* inconsistent. This presumption too is to be resisted. Where '*P*' contains non-logical elements essentially, there can be no proof of it which does not also contain non-logical elements. Logic alone does not distinguish between 'profits are maximised under perfect competition at the point where marginal cost equals marginal revenue' and 'elephants are happiest in captivity when they drink as much as they eat'. Even the whiskered example of 'All bachelors are unmarried' can only be found contingent, without aid from a true statement defining a bachelor as an unmarried man. It is not the necessity just of Pythagoras' theorem which depends on non-logical elements but also that of 'Given the laws of logic, Euclid's axioms entail Pythagoras' theorem.'

The effect of making necessity prior to proof is to license *a posteriori* knowledge of necessary truths. Long before

[5] Pap and Quine put the case in a way I find wholly cogent in the places just cited. They also make the points in the next two paragraphs, although, while Pap uses them to defend Leibniz, Quine turns them against the whole analytic–synthetic distinction.

Pythagoras, it is said, farmers in the Nile delta used the relation among the sides of right-angled triangles to rechart their land holdings after the annual flood. Perhaps they had merely noticed a regularity in triangles of a particular proportion, say 3, 4, 5, and were merely generalising inductively. But that does them little credit; let us suppose they had a general rule for any right angled triangle but without a proof. Here they would know *a posteriori* that a proposition was true but without knowing that it was necessarily true. In general, I submit, whoever knows that '*P*' is necessarily true has *a priori* knowledge; but one need not know that '*P*' is necessarily true, to know that '*P*' is true. Hence, while allowing Leibniz that truths of fact are contingent, we will not wish to assume that only truths *of* fact are true *in* fact. The billiard champion and the professor of pure mechanics both know truths about the behaviour of the same balls. The professor has trumped experience with theory, provided the champion does not cast doubt on the scope of the theory's application.

The last four paragraphs are heavily dogmatic and should be taken with a pinch of salt. So, as at the end of chapter 3, I shall be speaking in the subjunctive. *If* there were sound epistemic grounds for treating necessity as a primitive concept and a necessary truth as one which applied in fact whenever its conditions were satisfied, then there would also be good grounds for the view of definitions which comes next. It is a huge *if* but I shall try at least to set a puzzle for those who cannot swallow it.

Without the missing theory of advantage in chess, strong players have an impressive *a posteriori* grasp of what some chess Euclid or Pythagoras will one day prove. But, even when the uncertainties of Kriegspiel are added, to show that necessity can coexist with ignorance, the analogy with the understanding of social action is still tenuous. So I shall try again, with a more appealing example of the role of concepts in analysing experience. The example is Steven Lukes' study of Power and I shall use it first as an instance of an attempt at a real definition and then as an excuse for comment on the notion of value-relevance. Lukes has conveniently provided a miniature (to use the chess players' term for a problem with very few pieces) and its topic is the concept involved in asserting that one agent has power over another.[6]

Lukes offers 'a conceptual analysis of power' and 'a view of power (that is a way of identifying it) which is radical in both the theoretical and political senses' (p. 9). He begins from what he calls The One-Dimensional View, which measures $A$'s power over $B$ by $A$'s victories over $B$ in actual, overt conflict. Here the typical arena is the battlefield, the boardroom, parliament, the courts or the public meeting. The issue is visibly before the house and the loser is got to do something he would not otherwise do. In more elaborate form this behavioural view has distinguished pluralist accounts of American politics, especially in those vintage years when the republic seemed so healthy, open and democratic. Lukes quotes Robert Dahl, whose focus on the overt shows itself, for example, in judging that, 'the independence, penetrability and heterogeneity of the various segments of the political stratum all but guarantee that any dissatisfied groups will find spokesmen in the political stratum'.[7]

But $A$ also has power over $B$, if $A$ can prevent $B$'s challenge from surfacing. Victory in covert conflict is at least as important a measure. Where tensions can be released, demands confused or opponents divided, conflict need never reach the agenda. This thought prompts The Two-Dimensional View, typified for Lukes by the work of Peter Bachrach and Morton Baratz. These authors cite Schnattschneider's dictum that 'organisation is the mobilisation of bias' and observe on their own account, 'to the extent that a person or group – consciously or unconsciously – creates or reinforces barriers to the public airing of policy conflicts, that person or group has power'.[8] They anatomise the concept into Coercion ($A$ secures $B$'s compliance by threat of deprivation), Influence ($A$ causes $B$

---

[6] *Power, A Radical View*, London, Macmillan, 1974. It is not Lukes' idea that he is attempting a real definition but I am perplexed by his own account of his aims.

[7] *Who Governs? Democracy and Power in an American City*, Yale, 1961, p. 93; quoted by Lukes on p. 36 of *Power*. See also Dahl's early paper, 'The Concept of Power', in *Behavioural Science* 2, 1957, pp. 201–5.

[8] *Power and Poverty. Theory and Practice*, New York, 1970, p. 8; quoted by Lukes on p. 16 of *Power*. This is a study of Baltimore. For the dictum see E. Schnattschneider, *The Semi-Sovereign People: A Realist's View of Democracy in America*, New York, 1960

to change his course of action without tacit or overt threat), Authority (*B* complies because he recognises that *A*'s command is reasonable in terms of his own values), Force (*A* strips *B* of the choice between compliance and non-compliance) and Manipulation (a species of Force where *B* complies without recognising the source or exact nature of the demand upon him). Thus when the ruling group in Baltimore uses a poverty programme to deflect the inchoate demands of black citizens, they are wielding power, by a definition which gives *A* power over *B* whenever *A* gets *B* to comply by whatever means.

Lukes' own Three-Dimensional View takes the others to task for their individualism. The mobilisation of bias is the work not just of individuals but also of forms of organisation. Moreover power can sometimes be so well wielded that not even covert conflict occurs. 'To assume that the absence of grievance equals genuine consensus is simply to rule out the possibility of false or manipulated consensus by definitional fiat' (p. 24). The measure of a false consensus is that it goes against the real interests of those manoeuvred into it. Where *B*'s real interests are unharmed, *A* is exercising not power but influence. Hence a radical view of power introduces real interests as a third dimension, where organisational pressures are also at work.

This sketch is too brief to let us ask whether Lukes is right but I hope it reveals just enough of his strategy. He is after the analysis of the concept of power best suited to understanding what relation holds between *A* and *B* when *A* has power over *B*. The best analysis will have typical advantages over its rivals. For instance it will apply more widely or more clearly, include more of the determinants and show their connections better, excel in simplicity and elegance. The competing views of power are attempts at an analysis of the concept. 'The three views we have been considering can be seen as alternative interpretations and applications of one and the same underlying concept of power, according to which *A* exercises power over *B* when *A* affects *B* in a manner contrary to *B*'s interests.' (p. 27) It is a strategy which raises harder epistemological questions than Lukes had space for.

The central one lurks in the phrase 'one and the same underlying concept of power'. If there is just one underlying concept, the book's thesis is irresistible. The competing views are in effect that $A$ exercises power over $B$ when –

(1) $A$ prevails over $B$ in overt conflict because of $A$'s actions.

(2) $A$ prevails over $B$ in overt or covert conflict because of $A$'s actions.

(3) $A$'s real interests prevail over $B$'s because of $A$'s actions. The two-dimensional view has a clear edge on the one-dimensional, provided we can know what counts as covert conflict. The three-dimensional has a clear edge over the two-dimensional, given that the notion of real interests is contained in the unitary underlying concept. Moreover it is very plausible to regard the engineering of consent as a form of power which may sometimes avoid conflict altogether and, at least in Lukes' eyes, questions about where $B$'s real interests in fact lie are empirical.

But how do we judge that there is one underlying concept, in particular one containing reference to real interests? We might be tempted to hope that it can be got by some kind of abstraction from the power relations actually to be found among men. There is an echo here of the old empiricist theory of abstract ideas, whereby general terms are held to name some representative or average property of the members of the class they denote. Thus 'blue' is the name of what blue things have in common, subject to whatever is done about the fact that blue things differ quite widely in colour. But this is an echo best ignored. It is not the genesis of the concept which matters but how we are to know the truth of a kind of theoretical proposition. Nor can 'power' be treated like 'blue', even supposing that the sense of 'blue' is as the theory of abstract ideas would have it. Treating 'power over' as the name of a representative or average relation among men would be like treating 'force' in chess as the name of such a relation among chess pieces. There would indeed be force, if the theory were true, but the existence of force is not a given fact to which the theory very properly corresponds. It is a fact whose existence depends on the truth of the theory. Equally, if it is a truth that power is exercised only against someone's real interests, it is not a truth written on the face of experience.

Perhaps it is all too plain that theoretical propositions defining concepts are not empirical hypotheses about what the concepts refer to. If so, we can regard that way of treating ideal types as closed. The point is a general one about theoretical terms – to test for the existence of something, we must know already what we are testing for the existence of. The empirical scope of a concept can vary from place to place and the kinds of power exercised may differ from China to Peru. But empirical scope arises after the concept has been defined and given criteria of application. We should not ignore the necessity attached to the proposition that $A$ exercises power over $B$ when $A$ affects $B$ in a manner contrary to $B$'s interests.

What kind of proposition is it then? It seems to be a definition. But it is not a definition-in-use, since, on the evidence of Lukes' own argument, it is not the definition used by any of those whose view of power he regards as mistaken. It is not even in underlying use (to coin a phrase), unless the rejected authors are merely stupid and unreflective. Besides, there can hardly be anything sacred about usage in a young science constantly trying to improve its usages. Nor can it be a stipulative definition, since even a short book would be too long, if only stipulation were needed. And a precising definition, which refines an existing term, is a blend of stipulation and definition-in-use, which adds nothing of epistemological note to either. A persuasive definition cannot be what Lukes wants even for what he calls 'an essentially contested concept' (p. 26) and even granting him that rival definitions of power have different implications for ethics. He is not trying to engineer the consent of his readers by any old means but leading them by reasoned argument to see that his account extends the range of the concept's application 'further and deeper than others'. Since we have just listed all the sorts of definition recognised by orthodox empiricism, the plot thickens.

We reached a similar impasse in chapter 3, where the natural necessity in causal connections was presented as a conceptual necessity in statements of causal connections. A case was sketched for what used to be called 'real' definitions, true statements expressing the essence of the concept or thing defined. Lukes' book makes sense, to my mind, only as an attempt at a real definition of 'power over' and I see no other way to read a claim that a three-dimensional view goes deeper than the others. For instance critics will no doubt complain that $A$ can exercise power over $B$ in $B$'s real interests. It may be in the garrison's real interests to surrender because their lives will in fact be spared and because peace will in fact be used for the common good. It is in their interests whether they know it or not but the attacker has power over them, whatever fate he has in store for them. Lukes has to dispute the possibility. He might rule it out on the ground that the garrison have an overriding interest in their autonomy which is about to be violated; but he prefers to say that 'if and when $B$ recognises his real interests, the power relation ends: it is self-annihilating' (p. 33). In other words it is a case not of power but of influence. The critics will protest that what grows out of the barrel of even a friendly, neighbourhood gun is still power; that such a way with counter-examples smacks of abolishing the Oxford slums by redrawing the city boundaries. Lukes will have to prove them mistaken, Never mind whether he can. My point is that the exercise can be understood only as an attempt to show what is essential to a relation rightly classified as 'power over'.

The case for real definitions applies in any science where theory regulates descriptions of experience and does not just record and file them. It starts by noting that facts cannot be regarded as the referents of theory-free observation statements and that the paradigmatic theoretical statements, used to introduce primitive concepts, serve to rule out counter-examples to the theory in advance. But there is then a large snag, when we demand that the statements of a sound theory be both defeasible and true. Newton's laws of motion or the neo-Classical laws of supply and demand are not disconfirmable, since their regulative function is to ensure that disconfirming instances have been wrongly classified. Their truth, if they are true, results from their being devices for introducing the right concepts, rightly specified. So they are defeasible only if there are objective criteria for the choice and specification of the right concepts. In other words I take recent philosophy of science to have shown that empirical judgements presuppose theoretical judgements but not to have abolished the need for truth in science. Although the danger of a nominalist or conventionalist line on the choice of theoretical terms is thereby stark, it is not clear how a conceptualist line avoids it. It can do so, I submit, only by making old-fashioned claims for the possibility of real definitions.

A common function of purely theoretical statements is to define what would happen *ceteris paribus* or under ideal conditions. Frictionless motion is a well-known instance. Here theoretical models are used to measure and explain actual departures from the ideal and there is an analogous case for insisting that the ideal conditions must be *truly* stated. Hence there is reason to think that all causal-cum-theoretical explanation (as we dubbed it in chapter 3) involves real definitions and ideal types. To that extent chess can serve as a study of scientific theorising in miniature. But it is not a reason which distinguishes between natural and social science. Having asserted the general independence of theory and theory-dependence of facts, what shall we say about the conceptual understanding special to the social world?

Lukes himself makes it crucial that the social sciences deal in 'essentially contested concepts', power being 'one of those concepts which is ineradicably value-dependent' (p. 26). But there is no call to connect theory-dependence with value-dependence, unless one supposes that, since experience does not dictate the right choice of theoretical concepts, the torch passes to ideology. No doubt the analysis of power – or, to pick almost at random, of capital, democracy, intelligence, equality, identity, exchange, utility or motivation – does have implications for ethics. No one who grants the ineradicable function of a model of man in social theory will be surprised. But it follows neither that these concepts are value-dependent nor that concepts in natural science are different. 'Value-dependent' has relativist overtones, making analysis relative to the ethical opinions of the user and, in truth, people do analyse concepts to suit themselves. That property is theft is a conceptual thesis little heard in the Conservative club. But natural science also raises questions of *cui bono* and I see no quick reason for thinking them inherently different. Moral valuation is one thing and theoretical evaluation another.

What, then, is special to theoretical evaluation in social science? It is, I submit, that social scientists are conceptualising skill. Actors have natural, social and rational powers, whereas the sciences of nature are concerned only with powers of the first kind. Thus the genetic effects of thalidomide depend on the powers of the drug and the task of theory is to isolate these powers with models to distinguish lawlike from unlawlike connections. The actions of Themistocles, by contrast, depend also on two further kinds of powers. This is not to deny that natural powers, both his and those of people and things about him, come into it. But he also had the powers conferred by being the Athenian general facing a Persian invasion. These were partly those of a social position which enabled some courses of action while constraining others, partly those of command over a fleet of ships against a Persian force of mixed talent far from home and partly those of the respect which his fellows might not have given a different incumbent of his position. These natural and social powers were premises of a calculation whose outcome depended on his rational powers. History credits him with a nice judgement of what it was best to do, given his own capacity to carry it out, and Salamis has always had a place among the great naval victories. If it was truly thanks to him not only that the Athenians won it but also that they fought it at all, instead of defending Athens, and had the ships to fight it in, instead of using the product of the Laurium silver mines in other ways, then skill is a crucial factor.

To isolate the notion of skill, it is simplest to treat all other powers as premises and the skill as the passage to a conclusion. I have it in mind that what is called an economic or game-theoretic explanation of action should be seen as an ideal inference to a rational decision from premises in which societal concepts occur essentially. The actor's problem is specific to both what and whom he is and, being thus enabled and constrained, he has a range of options, each with consequences. These are the premises and there is a preliminary skill in

identifying them, since options may be hidden and consequences elusive. But the conclusion of a practical syllogism is
not so much an action as a reason for action. It is a statement of
what, in that case, it would be rational to do and such statements are hard to come by. Anyone who doubts it has only to
ask an economist what the government should do to combine
full employment with high real incomes.

The analogy with chess now looks promising again. The
grandmaster's problem arises only because he is playing a
game under rules which give him 'rights' and 'duties'. It is
posed by an opponent, whose skill is itself a factor in the
calculation. Its solution is one among several permitted
options, whose merits are hard to evaluate, and it calls for a
true theory of advantage in chess. The true theory idealises the
skill in a set of necessary truths whose essential concepts, like
'force', 'space' and 'time' are not in the rule-book. It is prescriptive and explains why inferior moves are inferior. It is
descriptive in so far as the master applies it. The rules define
the social powers and supply the premises; the theory defines
the skill and supplies the answers. But chess is still too narrow
a model. It is, after all, a 'one-dimensional' game, where $A$'s
various powers give him power over $B$, if $A$ can beat $B$ in overt
conflict. Kriegspiel adds a dimension, since the stronger player
manipulates information and can deny the weaker the overt
contest which the weaker might then win. But the modest
goal of both games is specified in the rules and no question of
ultimate interests arises.

So let us brave the third dimension by continuing with
sociology and economics. Consider a proposition from the
neo-Classical theory of demand – 'Given the theory of utility,
if there are substitutes for a good and other things are equal,
then, if its price rises, demand for it will fall.' What has this to
do with *a priori* knowledge in general and with the notion of
skill in particular? Well, firstly, it is best construed, I think, as a
necessary truth (or claimant to the title). Some will take it as a
putative law holding empirically for large numbers (and so not
upset by the odd exception). But it would then be vulnerable
to a charge of tautology, arising because the theory of utility
ensures that the consumer who ignores a price rise, *ceteris*

*paribus*, has an indifference map which makes it rational to do so. If the charge sticks – and I think it does – the only move short of dropping the proposition is to regard it as none the worse for being a tautology. 'Tautology' is not a term of abuse, if the arguments here and in chapter 3 are sound, provided that utility theory does more than record our determination to use economic words in one of several equally licit ways. Secondly, however, any way of dealing with exceptions which makes the proposition a necessary causal-cum-theoretical law about rational consumers also assigns it to a passive conception of man. An active conception differs by making it a proposition about skill. Given the theory of utility, if there are substitutes for a good and other things are equal, then, if its price rises, *there is good reason to buy less of it*. It is again necessarily true, if true at all, but ceases to be causal.

Its truth is no easier to establish on this rendering than on the other. Whether it is rational to buy less on those conditions depends on the soundness of utility theory, a complex matter which I leave to others. My point is solely that economic theory offers an exemplar for the validation of statements about the rational thing to do and one which suits Autonomous Man very well. But it does so only if the analogy with chess is not made too exact. Utility theory must not be a device for isolating what is rational from social considerations. In giving sociology the premises and economics the inference, I did not mean that what is economically *zweckrational* is therefore also finally rational. In chess, whose goal is defined by the rules, no player can doubt that a move which delivers mate is the best move. In a three-dimensional world we can indeed doubt whether it is rational to do what is economically *zweckrational*.

It may not be at all rational, for instance, to maximise profit in the market. To this neo-Classical economists (who usually agree) have various retorts. The most ambitious is that, although man is truly economic man, what counts is not profit in the market but utility; and, if a man's utility is better maximised by becoming a monk, then that tells economists something about his indifference map. Relatedly, when it comes to explaining actual behaviour, there is the option of using satisficing in place of maximising models, the difference being that the satisficer desists when he has enough, while the maximiser continues until he has as much as possible. Here, I think, satisficing is maximising some disjunction of more sorts of satisfaction than a hard boiled Benthamite would recognise. Or, more modestly, the economist may grant that man has other goals than those of economic man and so make what is rational depend on who and what the actor happens to be. In that case an analogous point arises, if the sociologist maintains that what is rational for a king is therefore rational for the man who is the king. The exact retort does not matter here, provided a link with chapters 5 and 6 is preserved and *Zweckrationalität* is not allowed to usurp questions of real interests. In leaving the soundness of utility theory to others, I did not mean only to economists. It has always been a theory of ethics.

That said, however, I do suggest that economists have ways of conceptualising skill so as to make Autonomous Man a subject for science. Equally theories of advantage in games of skill illustrate the kind of knowledge needed for understanding with the aid of ideal types. The best move is necessarily the best and the scientist need not know *a priori* that it is necessarily the best before knowing *a posteriori* that it is actually the best. *A posteriori* he is only laying bets but he must lay them, since the division of labour between active and passive explanations depends on it. If the actor is autonomous when he is rational and plastic when he is not, all hangs on our judging what would be the rational thing to do. Natural science is spared such judgements and this is the epistemological difference.

# 9

# *Envoi: actor and context*

Plastic Man started the book strongly placed. Nature and nurture were simple ideas but capable of the subtlest refinement. They could be filled out not only technically with models from cybernetics, statistics, economics and other realms of sophistication but also philosophically, in support of many divisions of labour between nature and nurture. Free action could be distinguished from unfree in ways congenial to some philosophers of mind, with familiar results in ethics and politics. The axis of strength was that all processes of action were seen as causally connected and so explicable with the best accounts of this relation to be had from the natural sciences and their philosophy. The one clear doubt was that Plastic Man, being but the intersection of a complex of laws, was not much of an individual. But perhaps the demand for a holier uniqueness was born of an unreflecting or socially generated individualism. At any rate the contrary thesis – that action has determinants unique to the agent–*an-sich* – was too cryptic to be cogent. In this epilogue I want to ask how he stands now and to end with a query about the notion of context.

Autonomous Man was ushered in with the thought that social action occurs on a stage built of shared meanings and norms. That might be awkward for behaviourists and for very mechanical accounts of how nature and nurture operate but it posed no general threat to Plastic Man. Indeed, by cashing the metaphor of the stage in terms of normative expectations attached to social positions and by letting *homo psychologicus* act within constraints on *homo sociologicus*, a passive conception did very nicely. An active conception started to emerge only when the thesis that motives were causes of action was contrasted with the claim that reasons were the explanation but not the cause of rational action. Fully rational action was its own explanation, given the context and the actor's identity. Context enabled and constrained, setting him problems because he was who he was. Rational action was a skill, not a pleonasm in the logic-of-the-situation-as-he-saw-it, and shortcomings were for causal explanation. His identity was a difficult hybrid of 'private' self and social 'self', the point being that atomic, pre-social individuals had no essential interests by which to judge which ends were rational, while the ends accruing to occupants of social positions were their rational ends only in a Good Society.

What could decide between these rival metaphysics? The crux was whether rational explanation was a special mode. Accepting the piety that the actors' world must be understood from within, we raised the Other Minds problem as one of understanding the actors' language. To get a bridgehead, the Enquirer had to make assumptions, centrally that communication was an activity among rational men. The assumption could fail in part – otherwise a viciously circular relativism set in – but it had to succeed in part and could fail only in ways which preserved the objective criteria of rationality. So an active conception of man always had the first move and causal explanations were needed only when it did not also have the last. Similarly, the actor's own reasons being the alpha of explanation, even when they were not also the omega, explanation in terms foreign to the actor was posterior and applied only to departures from rationality. This making of the rational prior to the real, or of the ideal prior to the actual, grounded a case for deeming theoretical judgements substantive and knowledge of their truth finally *a priori*. Those unconvinced earlier that the same went for every abstract scientific theory, were invited to allow judgements of rationality a special claim, peculiar to sciences which conceptualise skill.

Autonomous Man has first claim, then, since social action can be understood only as the rational expression of intention within rules. But he need not also have the last. Between alpha and omega, where models of rational action give advice which

186

actors do not follow and call for skills which they do not have, two kinds of explanation co-exist. The compromise no doubt sets puzzles unresolved here but I cannot end without touching on a further conundrum. It concerns the notion of context.

So far context has usually been treated as all of a piece, on the analogy of the rules of chess in relation to the moves played. But that will not do, partly because natural context is unlike the rules of chess and partly because social context is not always complete and external. Natural context is more relevant than has emerged. Social life has a natural setting, imperfectly mastered and, like other contexts, both enabling and constraining. It matters to social action that we live on a planet with grass and uranium, rain and volcanoes, baboons and bacteria; that our species seeks food, shelter, sex and conversation, is prone to disorder, able to laugh and blessed with opposable thumbs; that our fellows differ in strength, colour and wits. There is only a loose distinction between natural and social – the question, 'Discuss the importance of being the right shape and size' has been set by examiners in biology and in sociology. The state of technology, for instance, as vital to the history of religion as of physics, depends on what there is to know about nature, on what is actually known, and on what it is socially permitted to know. But, however loose the distinction, natural context makes a difference and cannot simply be swept up into a stock of shared meanings.

That noted, however, my closing query has to do with social context, with the rules, requirements, permissions and sanctions which hedge the actor trying to pursue his own good in his own way. Single actors on single occasions may be bound by rules which are external and complete in the short run. Yet even here there is often latitude. The actor has some choice of legitimate goals and interpretations, like a sculptor hired to produce £10,000 of large art for the town square. Also overt conformity to rules is often a poor guide to what is afoot, as when secret agents use the Deaths columns of *The Times* for sending coded messages. With several actors and in the longer run the metaphor of a fixed stage grows ever more misleading. The rules do not apply uniformly and they alter. In part this is uncontentiously owing to place and time, with the *mores* of

Tooting being the jest of Hampstead and with loyalty to the crown becoming treason to the State. But I have it more in mind that actors have a power to alter rules collectively which they lack singly. This power is an emergent property and it sets a problem for a book like this, which considers single actions by single actors with the presumption that what is typical is also true in general.

For a single actor institutions are usually given, being stores of power and stocks of reasons for action. He can count on being helped or hindered, depending on what he decides to do, and this fact is a reason which influences his decision. The same picture can be used for small groups trying to change an institution – for instance for a campaign against the abortion laws – provided there are larger institutions as a given context. But it cannot be used when the actors are the institution, for example when writing the history of the Soviet communist party after it had taken power. Once the actors can change the rules which enable and constrain them, context shifts from partial *explanans* to *explanandum*. Often, no doubt, the initiative is not perceived or not taken but an active conception of society cannot accept that there is always enough of a given context to let the explanation of each action serve as model for the explanation of all. That is why the social contract myth is so tantalising – it is the ideal type of situation where the action is supposed to explain the rules but where it is hard to see how the action could be rational without a stock of reasons to draw on. But less mythical cases are common. Where, for instance, a single Catholic decides his attitude to the church's attitude on contraception, Catholics collectively decide the church's attitude itself. The difference is not just one between tactics and strategy, since the identity of the group is involved. We asked earlier how a man can rationally choose the roles which determine who he essentially is. Analogously, can a group rationally decide the beliefs and purposes which define it? If not, the alpha of social explanation does not apply to institutional action.

It could be held that there is always enough of a context to make changes of group identity rational over time. For instance churches do manage to embrace heresies once deemed

188

so major that a change of identity is involved. But they do not do so at one swoop. There are years of debate, aided by external events, and each step is a small, rational movement, even if the last contradicts the first. The Lutherans began with a central doctrine of submission to political rulers of whatever stripe and came to advocate resistance, while still remaining the same church.[1] Undoubtedly it happens. But the conceptual puzzle is not removed by spreading it thinly over years and the question is whether we must make the best of a bad job. If a group which essentially believes $P$ can come rationally to believe $not$-$P$, then the historian seems to have four options. Firstly, he may maintain that, thanks to the changing situation, $P$ does not conflict with $not$-$P$. This indeed disposes of the particular case but it leaves the general problem standing, since we can hardly prove that no group ever changes its identity. Secondly he may find that the group had no sufficient reason to believe $P$ originally. But in that case rational explanation fails just where it ought to begin, if rational man models are also to be the key to institutional action. Thirdly he may point out, plausibly enough, that changes of belief can be rational without having the form of logically rigorous arguments. Thus, Lutheran political theory formally entailed neither submission nor resistance but contained the makings of a rational case for either. But now rational explanation is *eo ipso* incomplete since it cannot explain why a group with reason to believe $P$ comes to believe $not$-$P$ for no better reason; in so far as the original doctrine defined the group, it stands as a reason for not taking each little step away from it and, the greater the distance gone, the stronger the reason. Fourthly, mindful perhaps of those charities for the relief of Crimean veterans which flourish long after the last veteran is dead, he may agree that a new group has replaced the old. But, as a general solution, that would make intellectual history too precarious and multiply the number of units without discovering how to deal with any of them. Pragmatically, no doubt, a judicious

---

[1] I take the example from Quentin Skinner's monumental *Foundations of Modern Political Thought*, forthcoming from the Cambridge University Press, where this problem is very much to the fore. Skinner has many other examples and the intellectual historian's problems of rational explanation are deeply pondered in his introductory chapter.

blend of options will let the historian tell a plausible yarn and only a poor student of mankind would ask for more. Conceptually, however, we were hoping for a notion of rational action to apply to the collective creation of context as well as to individuals acting within context. No option yields one.

It is too late in this short book to aim at a theory of power institutions and collective action for Autonomous Man and I freely admit to relief. Hence the compromise between active and passive which gives active the alpha and passive the omega also leaves passive theories better placed to account for institutions. We do have an active explanation of how actors can bend the rules and combine to make limited changes within a larger context. But institutions seem to me more than the results, foreseen and unforeseen, of individual negotiations. A theory of emergence is needed, I think, and then a final recipe for the Good Society which lets us judge whether an institution serves human interests. But, even without knowing the eternal truths, we have a case for some small ones. In particular, I submit, there is no doing without a model of man and, whatever the merits of rationalism, there is no shirking the great hypotheses which divide metaphysicians.

# Bibliography

The books are those I have had most in mind in writing the text. Stars mark the ones which seem to me to offer most to anyone in unfamiliar terrain, The books are followed by a selection of useful anthologies.

## Books

Achinstein, P., *Law and Explanation*, Oxford University Press, 1971.

*Arrow, K., *Social Choice and Individual Values*, London, 1951.

*Aune, B., *Rationalism, Empiricism and Pragmatism*, New York, Random House, 1970.

*Ayer, A. J., *Language, Truth and Logic*, London, Gollancz, 1936.
   *Philosophical Essays*, London, Macmillan, 1954.
   *The Origins of Pragmatism*, London, Macmillan, 1968.

*Barry, B., *Sociologists, Economists and Democracy*, London, Macmillan, 1970.

*Berger, P., *Invitation to Sociology*, Penguin, 1966.

Berger, P. and Luckman, T., *The Social Construction of Reality*, London, Allen Lane, 1967.

Bhaskar, R., *A Realist Theory of Science*, Leeds, Leeds Books, 1975.

Bradley, F. H., *Ethical Studies*, Oxford, 1876, reprinted 1962.

*Braithwaite, R. B., *Scientific Explanation*, Cambridge, CUP, 1953.

Burrow, J., *Evolution and Society*, Cambridge, CUP, 1966.

Chomsky, N., *Language and Mind*, New York, Harcourt, 1968.

*Collingwood, R., *The Idea of History*, Oxford, Clarendon, 1936.

*Dahrendorf, R., *Homo Sociologicus*, London, Routledge, 1973.

Dewey, John, *Human Nature and Conduct*, New York, 1922.

Douglas, J. D., *The Social Meanings of Suicide*, Princeton UP, 1967.

Downs, A., *An Economic Theory of Democracy*, New York, 1947.

*Dray, W. H., *Laws and Explanation in History*, OUP, 1957.

191

*Durkheim, E., *The Rules of Sociological Method*, Glencoe, Ill., The Free Press, 1965.

*Suicide: A Study in Sociology*, London, Routledge, 1952.

*The Elementary Forms of the Religious Life*, London, Allen and Unwin, 1915.

Emmet, D. M., *Rules, Roles and Relations*, London, 1966.

Evans-Pritchard, E. E., *Witchcraft, Oracles and Magic Among the Azande*, Oxford, Clarendon, 1937.

*Friedman, M., *Essays in Positive Economics*, chapter 1, Chicago, Chicago UP, 1966.

Gardiner, P., *The Nature of Historical Explanation*, OUP, 1968.

Gellner, E., *Thought and Change*, London, Weidenfeld, 1965.

*Legitimation of Belief*, Cambridge, CUP, 1975.

*Goffman, E., *The Presentation of Self in Everyday Life*, New York, Doubleday, 1959.

*Relations in Public*, Penguin, 1971.

*Frame Analysis*, Penguin, 1974.

Goldman, A. I., *A Theory of Human Action*, Prentice-Hall, 1970.

Gouldner, A. W., *The Coming Crisis of Western Sociology*, London, Heinemann, 1971.

Habermas, J., *Knowledge and Human Interests*, London, Heinemann, 1972.

Harré, R. and Madden, E. J., *Causal Powers: A Theory of Natural Necessity*, Oxford, Blackwell, 1975.

Harré, R. and Secord, P., *The Explanation of Social Behaviour*, Oxford, Blackwell, 1972.

*Hart, H. L. A. and Honore, A. M., *Causation and the Law*, London, OUP, 1959.

Hempel, C. G., *Aspects of Scientific Explanation*, Glencoe, The Free Press, 1965.

*Philosophy of Natural Science*, Prentice-Hall, 1966.

Hesse, M. B., *Models and Analogies in Science*, London, Sheed and Ward, 1963.

*The Structure of Scientific Inference*, London, Macmillan, 1974.

Hollis, M. and Nell, E. J., *Rational Economic Man*, Cambridge, CUP, 1975.

Homans, G., *The Nature of Social Science*, New York, Harcourt, 1967.

James, W., *The Principles of Psychology*, 1890, Dover Books, 1950.

* *Psychology: Briefer Course*, Collier Books, 1962.

Keat, R. and Urry, J., *Social Theory as Science*, London, Routledge, 1975.

Kenny, A. J. P., *Action, Emotion and the Will*, London, Routledge, 1963.

*Will, Freedom and Power*, Blackwell, 1975.

Koopmans, T., *Three Essays on the State of Economic Science*, New York, McGraw-Hill, 1957.

Körner, S., *Categorial Frameworks*, Oxford, Blackwell, 1970.

*Kuhn, T., *The Structure of Scientific Revolutions*, Chicago, Chicago UP, 1970.

Laing, R. S., *The Divided Self*, London, Penguin, 1965.

Lessnoff, M., *The Structure of Social Science*, London, Allen and Unwin, 1974.

Lewis, C. I., *Mind and the World Order*, 1929, Dover Books, 1956.

Lewis, D., *Convention: a Philosophical Study*, Harvard University Press, 1969.

*Lipsey, P. E., *Introduction to Positive Economics*, Harper and Row, 1972.

Louch, A., *Explanation and Human Action*, Oxford, Blackwell, 1967.

Lukes, S., *Power, A Radical View*, London, Macmillan, 1974.

Mackie, J. L., *The Cement of the Universe*, Oxford, 1974.

MacIntyre, A., *Against the Self-Images of the Age*, London, Duckworth, 1971.

*Mannheim, K., *Ideology and Utopia*, London, Routledge, 1966.

Mead, G. H., *Mind, Self and Society*, University of Chicago Press, 1934.

*Melden, A. I., *Free Action*, London, Routledge, 1961.

Merton, R. K., *Social Theory and Social Structure*, New York, 1957.

*Mill, J. S., *A System of Logic*, London, Longmans, 1961.

von Mises, L., *Human Action*, London, William Hodge, 1949.

*Epistemological Problems of Economics*, Princeton, 1960.

*Nadel, S., *The Theory of Social Structure*, London, Routledge, 1957.

Nagel, E., *The Structure of Science*, London, Routledge, 1961.

Olson, M., *The Logic of Collective Action*, Cambridge, Mass., 1965.

*Peters, R. S., *The Concept of Motivation*, Routledge, 1970.

*Popper, K., *The Poverty of Historicism*, London, Routledge, 1957.

*The Logic of Scientific Discovery*, London, 1959.

*Conjectures and Refutations*, London, 1963.

*Objective Knowledge*, Oxford, 1972.

Quine, W. v. O., *From a Logical Point of View*, Harvard University Press, 1961.

*Word and Object*, MIT Press, 1960.

*The Ways of Paradox*, New York, 1966.

Rawls, J., *A Theory of Justice*, Harvard University Press, 1971.

Richards, D. A. J., *A Theory of Reasons for Action*, Oxford, Clarendon, 1971.

Riker, W. H. and Ordeshook, P. C., *An Introduction to Positive Political Theory*, Englewood Cliffs, 1973.

Robbins, L., *An Essay on the Nature and Significance of Economic Science*, Macmillan, 1932, 2nd edition 1935.

Rudner, R., *Philosophy of Social Science*, Prentice-Hall, 1966.

Runciman, W., *Sociology in its Place*, Cambridge, CUP, 1970.

*A Critique of Max Weber's Philosophy of Social Science*, Cambridge, CUP, 1972.

*Ryan, A., *The Philosophy of the Social Sciences*, London, Macmillan, 1970.

Schutz, A., *The Phenomenology of the Social World*, London, 1972.

Simon, H. A., *Models of Man*, Wiley and Sons, 1957.

*Administrative Behavior*, New York, Free Press, 1945, 2nd edition with introduction, 1957.

*Skinner, B. F., *Beyond Freedom and Dignity*, London, Penguin, 1973.

Skinner, Q., *The Foundations of Modern Political Thought*, Cambridge University Press (forthcoming).

Strawson, P. F., *Individuals*, London, Methuen, 1959.

*Taylor, C., *The Explanation of Behaviour*, London, 1964.

Weber, M., *The Methodology of the Social Sciences*, New York, Macmillan, 1950.

*The Theory of Social and Economic Organisation*, Glencoe, Free Press, 1964.

*Roscher and Knies: the Logical Problems of Historical Economics*, New York, Free Press, 1975.

Whorf, B. L., *Language, Thought and Reality*, ed. J. B. Carroll, MIT Press, 1956.

Williams, B. A. O., *Problems of the Self*, Cambridge, CUP, 1973.

*Winch, P., *The Idea of a Social Science*, London, 1958.

von Wright, G. H., *Explanation and Understanding*, New York, Cornell UP, 1971.

Zetterberg, H. L., *On Theory and Verification in Sociology*, Ottawa, 1968.

## Anthologies

Benn, S. I. and Mortimore, G. W., eds, *Rationality and the Social Sciences*, London, Routledge, 1976.

Borger, R. and Cioffi, F., eds, *Explanation in the Behavioural Sciences*, Cambridge, CUP, 1970.

Braybrooke, D., ed., *Philosophical Problems of Social Science*, New York and London, Macmillan, 1965.

Brodbeck, M., ed., *Readings in the Philosophy of the Social Sciences*, New York, Macmillan, 1968.

Douglas, M., ed., *Rules and Meanings, The Anthropology of Everyday Knowledge*, Penguin, 1973.

Dray, W., ed., *Philosophical Analysis and History*, New York, Harper and Row, 1966.

Emmet, D. and MacIntyre, A., eds, *Sociological Theory and Philosophical Analysis*, London, Macmillan, 1970.

Gardiner, P., ed., *Theories of History*, London, Allen and Unwin, 1960.

* *The Philosophy of History*, Oxford, OUP, 1974.

Giddens, A., ed., *Sociology and Philosophy*, London, Heinemann, 1973.

*Positivism and Sociology*, London, Heinemann, 1974.

Hook, S., ed., *Philosophy and History*, New York, NYUP, 1963.

Lakatos, I. and Musgrave, A., eds, *Criticism and the Growth of Knowledge*, Cambridge, CUP, 1970.

Laslett, P., *et al.*, eds, *Philosophy, Politics and Society*, Series I—IV, Oxford, Blackwell, 1956–72.

Natanson, M., ed., *Philosophy of the Social Sciences*, New York, Random House, 1953.

Nidditch, P., ed., *Philosophy of Science*, Oxford, The Clarendon Press, 1968.

O'Neill, J., ed., *Modes of Individualism and Collectivism*, London, Heinemann, 1973.

*Ryan, A., ed., *The Philosophy of Social Explanation*, Oxford, OUP, 1973.

Wallace, W., ed., *Sociological Theory*, Heinemann, 1969.

Wilson, B., ed., *Rationality*, Oxford, Blackwell, 1970.

# Index of names